A DINING ROOM in a Fife villa and a bedroom in a Highland croft house . . . the library built for a wealthy banker and the star-filled ceiling of an island palace . . . Robert Louis Stevenson's bathroom and the plush Victorian bar where he might have dined. . . .

Widely differing interiors like these represent the heart of Scotland's heritage. Castles, country houses, cottages, tenements, terraces and villas — as far flung as Wester Ross and the Borders — are all represented in the SCOTTISH INTERIORS COLLECTION.

Other volumes will be available at three-monthly intervals and include Scottish Early Interiors, Scottish Georgian Interiors and Scottish Edwardian Interiors, which, with Scottish Victorian Interiors comprise the SCOTTISH INTERIORS COLLECTION. The four volumes cover four centuries of Scottish interior decoration.

Each of the interiors featured in this series is very much lived-in today, and we are indebted to their owners whose generosity has made it possible to invite readers into their homes through these pages. In addition, each volume features a National Trust for Scotland property, which readers can visit themselves, as well as the home of a member of the Historic Houses Association for Scotland, some of which are also open to the public.

SCOTTISH VICTORIAN INTERIORS features seven interiors as well as articles to guide the enthusiastic reader wishing to recreate elements of the many styles of the era, with lists of where to go to obtain furnishings, fittings and finishings.

Most of Scotland's traditional housing stock is Victorian but few homes retain original furnishings and fittings to anything like the extent of Ivy Jardine's Cardy House at Lower Largo or David Liddell-Grainger's Ayton Castle in Berwickshire. For different reasons, no other Victorian interiors are like Donald Mackenzie's thatched croft house in Wester Ross, or the Marquess of Bute's home, Mount Stuart near Rothesay. These interiors have been photographed in colour for the first time in this volume.

We hope you will enjoy exploring the interiors in the pages which follow and that you might even take ideas and inspiration from them to apply to your own home — and, of course, that you will find a permanent space on your bookshelves for the entire SCOTTISH INTERIORS COLLECTION.

National Trust for Scotland properties open to the public which contain Victorian interiors, or Victorian elements, include: Fyvie Castle, Brodick Castle, Falkland Palace, Brodie Castle, Haddo House, Angus Folk Museum, Hugh Miller's Cottage, Barrie's Birthplace, Carlyle's Birthplace, Castle Fraser.
Historic Houses Association for Scotland Members' houses with Victorian interiors or elements which are open to the public include: Ayton Castle, Bowhill, Braemar Castle, Dalmeny House, Dunrobin Castle, Floors Castle, Glamis Castle, Thirlestane Castle, Torosay Castle.
For further details about the National Trust for Scotland see page 66.
For information about the Historic Houses Association contact the Association's central office at 38 Ebury Street, London SW1W 0LU.

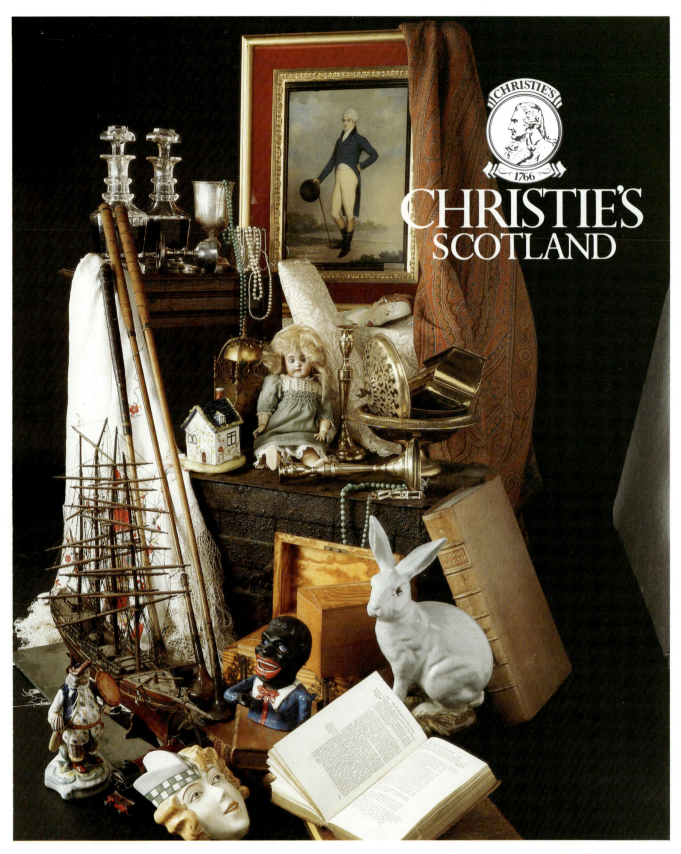

A fortune in your attic . . . And not a Renoir in sight.

CONTENTS

Above: *detail of wall painting at Ayton Castle, Berwickshire, by Bonnar & Carfrae, 1872.*

SCOTTISH VICTORIAN INTERIORS

MOUBRAY HOUSE PRESS
in association with
The National Trust for Scotland
And
Historic Houses Association
ISBN 0 948473 04 5

Editor — Sheila Mackay
Series Consultant — Ian Gow
Sub-editor — Jeremy Bruce-Watt

Publisher — Nic Allen
Design — Dorothy Steedman at Graphic Partners
Photography — Douglas MacGregor

Advertising Associate — Margaret Wilson
Classified Advertising — Margaret Clezy
Advertising Design — Ros King

Administrative Assistant — Anne Whitaker

MOUBRAY HOUSE PRESS, 53 High Street, Edinburgh EH1 1SR Tel 031-556 4402 Copyright 1986

Colour Separations by Marshall Thompson, Edinburgh. Printed by The Allen Lithographic Company, Kirkcaldy. Binding by Hunter & Foulis Ltd., Edinburgh.

Moubray House Press wishes to thank the owners of the houses featured in SCOTTISH VICTORIAN INTERIORS: Marquess of Bute, Brian Donkin, Lady Dunpark, Ivy Jardine, David Liddell-Grainger, Donald Mackenzie and The National Trust for Scotland. Thanks are also due to Frank Barstow, Laurance Black, John Gifford, Harry Lindley, Joyce Mair, Jim Souness.

All photography by Douglas Macgregor except pp. 34, 35 (Nic Allen), pp. 62-65 (National Trust for Scotland), p. 79 (Michael McLaren), p. 80, 81 (Osborne & Little), p. 83 (Marston & Langinger), p. 83 (Paris Ceramics), p. 84 (Sekers Ltd), p. 84 (Dave Williams).

The following photographs are reproduced by kind permission of The People's Palace Museum, pp. 6-9, Royal Commission on the Ancient and Historical Monuments of Scotland pp. 11, 13, 15, 16, 19, 69, 88, 89, Mrs J. Newall p. 12.

Front Cover. The library at Ayton Castle.
*Back Cover. **Above left:** bedroom at Cardy House, Lower Largo; **above right:** stained glass windows, Café Royal, Edinburgh; **below left:** bedroom, No. 12 Lower Ardelve, Wester Ross, **below right:** bathroom, Heriot Row, Edinburgh.*
Photography by Douglas MacGregor.

SMALLBONE
HANDMADE KITCHENS

*Old Pine in a country cottage: To give the warm glow of old pine, timbers,
often over 100 years old, are carefully prepared to retain
their original patina.*

At our beautiful showroom in the heart of Edinburgh you can experience the special atmosphere of genuine Smallbone kitchens and bedrooms. We have proved ourselves the leading designers, manufacturers and fitters of hand crafted, fitted kitchens and bedrooms. Choose from Old Pine, Oak or Hand-painted Kitchens and Chestnut and Hand-painted Bedrooms. A Smallbone designer can come to your home and create an individual design based on our unique concept.

26 CASTLE ST. EDINBURGH 031 225 8222

GLASGOW'S GLORIOUS GLASS

Michael Donnelly has rescued hundreds of jewel-like stained glass panels from the demolisher's hammer but despite growing public appreciation of the art form he still comes across precious examples in street markets like Glasgow's famous "Barras". Here he explains how the city's popular local history museum came to house the best collection of Victorian stained glass outside the Victoria and Albert Museum.

Michael Donnelly, assistant keeper of The People's Palace Museum, photographed in the Winter Gardens overlooking Glasgow Green.

In the white heat of the nineteenth century Industrial Revolution, Glasgow vied with Manchester for the title of industrial capital of the British Empire. Glasgow-made textiles, pottery, cast iron, marine and civil engineering were exported to all parts of the globe.

The end of the Empire meant the disappearance of renowned household names like Beardmore, Fairfield, John Brown, Arrol, Bell, Macfarlane and a thousand other companies which, through their well-crafted products, transformed the legend "Made in Glasgow" into an international testimonial of excellence.

As these great workshops vanished from the city, so too did most of their products. Today, only in the pillared hall of a Maharajah's palace or a South American railway station can one grasp the full achievement of Glasgow cast iron, while the great passenger liners which were Scotland's pride are now as exotic to new generations of Glaswegians as a space satellite. The product of only one industry in which Glasgow was for a time pre-eminent has survived in any significant quantity or quality in the city - stained glass.

Between 1870 and 1914 Glasgow became firmly established as one of the most important world centres for stained glass production. The reasons for the re-establishment of this ancient craft in Victorian Glasgow are many and complex. The rise of the shipbuilding industry was one important factor; but of equal significance was the disruption and schism within the Church of Scotland, with the resulting proliferation of churches. This provided a catalyst for architecture and the decorative arts in the mid-nineteenth century,

unparalleled until the post-war reconstruction of Germany under the Marshall Plan.

At the height of stained glass production in the 1890s, Glasgow had some thirty studios employing hundreds of skilled craftsmen and over one hundred artists. So prolific was their output that for a time stained glass outstripped sculpture and murals as the most democratic of art forms. In Glasgow it could be found in every kind of building from the private mansions and villas of the rich to the stairhead windows of the tenement closes. It could be found in pubs, restaurants, tearooms, libraries, town halls, in cinemas and public baths. It could be seen in police stations and Provosts' lamp posts, and above all in churches, chapels and synagogues.

Despite the sunshine window craze of the early 1960s and the concurrent fashion for flush-panelled doors, thousands of domestic doors and window panels containing stained glass survive today; so many, indeed, that they are generally taken for granted. Moreover, much is of a very high quality, precisely because the systematic destruction of medieval stained glass in Scotland meant that the best studios were saved from the worst effects of excessive historicism and production-line copying which gave Victorian stained glass elsewhere in Britain the bad reputation from which it still suffers.

Pioneering studio owners like James Ballantine of Edinburgh and John Cairney of Glasgow were well educated and accomplished

'Sunflowers' by Bruce J. Talbert. Cottier & Co. Studio for Colearn House, Auchterarder, 1872.

craftsmen with wide ranging cultural interests and contacts. While neither can be regarded as artists of real significance their methods of training and example laid the foundations of Scotland's excellence. In Ballantine's studio Frances Wilson Oliphant received an excellent grounding before embarking on a tragically short but highly prolific career as the friend and collaborator of the great presiding genius of the Gothic Revival, Augustus Welby Pugin. Later still the same studio launched the career of Stephen Adam, Scotland's leading designer of ecclesiastical stained glass between 1870 and his death in 1910.

In Glasgow, John Cairney trained a powerful triumvirate of designers in Daniel Cottier, Charles Gow and John Lamb Lyon who pioneered stained glass production in Australia. Indeed, in Cottier, Cairney had as an apprentice the finest all-round interior decorator to emerge in Scotland between the death of Robert Adam and the emergence of Charles Rennie Mackintosh. It would be hard to overstate the importance of Cottier to the development of decorative art in Scotland in all its aspects. As the pupil and later the rival of William Morris, Cottier became the catalyst and impresario for a highly gifted generation of Scottish artists at home and abroad, while his activities as a connoisseur and picture dealer influenced public taste in painting in Scotland, Australia and America.

By 1975 this tremendous outpouring of creative effort was largely forgotten and the stained glass industry had dwindled to the merest shadow of its former glory. Even in the Glasgow School of Art it had become a marginal subject for study.

In the People's Palace, which had featured cartoons

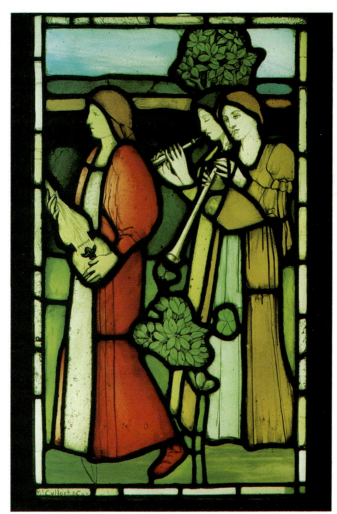

'Music' by David Gauld for McCulloch & Co., 1891. Private collection.

and sketches from many of the leading studios in its inaugural exhibition, the only evidence of stained glass as a local artefact (though not as a product) consisted of twenty panels of glass, depicting the Trades of the Burgh of Maryhill. These panels, dating from 1878 and designed by Stephen Adam, were rescued through the intervention of Bill Swinton, the District Council Clerk of Works. In the catalogue of exhibits they were wrongly identified as the work of the mysterious Adam C. Small.

Problems of identification are associated with the basic immobility of the medium and have always bedevilled the work of the stained glass artist. A stained glass window is composed of a mosaic of individually selected and painted pieces

of coloured glass, held together by strips of lead known as cames, and between creation and installation it is always vulnerable and difficult to display. Therefore an artist might produce his finest work for a private mansion and, after a public exhibition in a studio, perhaps for a week or two at the most, it disappeared from public view and memory. Most domestic windows are unsigned, and if an owner removed to a new home after a reverse or increase in fortune, the creator of the window would be forgotten by the new owner as well as the public.

It was for this reason that in 1978, in response to the increase in church demolition and the subdivision of former villas, I

decided to research the origins of Glasgow stained glass, turning my attention to the surviving records of the studios. I had become a curator at the People's Palace on Glasgow Green which was established in 1898 as an all-purpose cultural centre for the working classes. It owed its inception to a combination of the reforming zeal of late nineteenthth century Liberalism and the cultural and political evangelism of people like John Ruskin and William Morris. Since 1940 it has been the local history museum for the City of Glasgow. However, many of its acquisitions - notably the stained glass collection- are of recent origin and of national importance.

Most of the major studios had either closed down or abandoned stained glass production. However, some like J. & W. Guthrie and A. Wells Ltd. were still in business as interior decorators and had held on to a proportion of their sketch designs. In 1979-80 these were acquired by the museum and formed the foundation of an archive.

The search for artwork was assisted by the common practice in the glazing trade of studio inheritance, where newer firms occupied the premises of former studios. Another factor in my favour was the practice of sub-contracting, under which a common glazier would advertise his expertise with stained glass and then pass the job on to one of the established studios. In this way many significant caches of sketch designs produced for long-defunct studios were recovered on other premises.

In 1981 the People's Palace mounted a major exhibition of stained glass, featuring much of the recovered artwork and some forty individual panels of church and domestic glass rescued from derelict buildings or gifted by former

studios. The booklet accompanying the exhibition, entitled *Glasgow Stained Glass - A Preliminary Study*, deliberately emphasised the interim nature of its conclusions, since Glasgow - and indeed Scottish - stained glass is scattered throughout the world and has yet to be relocated and assessed.

In the 1980s the pace of church demolition has barely slackened and the collection of panels at the People's Palace has grown to over 200, making it the most comprehensive collection of Victorian stained glass in Britain outside the Victoria and Albert Museum. However, fortunately for us all, the best stained glass gallery is still in situ in the hundreds of public and private buildings for which it was designed. There has been a heartening increase in public awareness and appreciation of the heritage on our doorsteps. While we still lag a long way behind Germany and America in the field of conservation and public patronage of the arts, any change, however slight, is a sign of hope.

With the commitment and skill of veteran artists of the calibre of Sadie McLellan, John Blyth and Sax Shaw and the increasing involvement of young artists like Douglas Hogg, John Clark, Susan Bradbury, Paul Lucky, Shona McInnes and Susan Laidler, and the sympathetic consideration of architects and public bodies, Scottish stained glass can be assured of both an increasingly appreciated past and a worthwhile future.

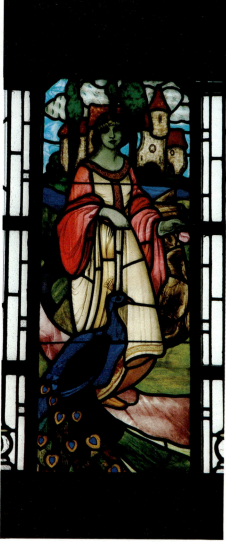

1 'The Gasworker' by Stephen Adam for Maryhill Burgh Halls, 1878, People's Palace Collections.
2 'Jason and the Golden Fleece' by Vincent Hart for Cottier & Co., 1880, People's Palace Collections.
3 'Water Sprite' by W. G. Morton, c1896, People's Palace Collections.
4 'Princess of the Peacocks'. Artist unknown. For St. Enoch's Glass Co., Glasgow. Private collection.

The People's Palace, Glasgow Green, is open daily 10-5pm; Sundays 2-5pm. Closed 25th December and 1st January.

SCOTS VICTORIANS AT HOME

One might be forgiven for expecting the Victorians' love of domesticity and enthusiastic commitment to photography to have left us with an intimate insight into their homes. In the early years, however, there were practical problems to be resolved in taking 'sun pictures' indoors, but even when these were mastered there is an impression that we are seeing only as much as they wished us to see. *Ian Gow* reveals some gems from the National Monuments Record of Scotland collection.

Most country houses still possess substantial photograph albums which record both their indoor and outdoor aspects. These views are often of such technical quality that if we take a magnifying glass to the large sepia prints, the prying modern eye can read the titles of the books they were reading and discover discarded needlework in the corner of a sofa. Alas however, there is little chance of finding anything improper, and then, as now, 'the lived-in look' was a carefully cultivated effect. As the sumptuous gilt and morocco bindings of the albums proclaim, photography was a luxury. The wealthy owners of these houses were careful to instruct their plentiful domestic servants to tidy the rooms before they were exposed to the gaze of a professional photographer.

The Victorians restricted the range of subjects deemed worthy of a photograph. Thus, while numerous photographers toiled before Mary Queen of Scots's bed at Holyrood, almost nobody thought a kitchen worth the trouble unless it had belonged to Robert Burns, and the dictates of propriety banned photographers from the bedroom floor.

At the end of the period technical innovations led to a broadening of the range of recorded interiors and the great age of interior photography came in the 1880s. Changes in both cameras and film made it possible for even an unskilled amateur to take 'snapshots' although few people bothered to survey their own homes. The Mather family showed great foresight in photographing the interior of 16 Leamington Terrace. Some of their results are included in this selection from the Record's collection.

When it became possible to reproduce photographs cheaply enough for periodicals, there was a spate of articles on historic houses. Since this coincided with the related interest in 'period' furniture, the results are rarely as naturalistic as they seem. All too often the photographer, in his enthusiasm for the 'old', would temporarily edit the furniture the family actually used out of camera range, in favour of a stiff line-up of Chippendale chairs. As one owner remarked after a visit from *Country Life,* the published result was "worse than having burglars".

16 LEAMINGTON TERRACE, EDINBURGH

Although these photographs may date from as late as 1905, they are selected from one of the most complete surveys yet discovered of a late Victorian town house. This belonged to Alexander Mather, who must have set up his married home here in the 1880s. The house was conveniently sited within walking distance of the works of 'Alexander Mather and Son, Millwrights, Engineers and Ironfounders' in Fountainbridge. Here he and his wife brought up their family of five daughters and a son. Their principal interest was music, and the children frequently performed as a sextet as their photograph album shows. It is not clear which member of the family was the photographer, but the ranks of photographs on the drawing room walls suggest it was a serious pursuit.

The photographs of their home are particularly interesting just because the Mathers were not specially interested in decoration. The overall effect is of several layers of taste. Some of the mid-Victorian furniture may have been inherited, like the ormolu mounted cabinet in the drawing room, and the parents' half-tester bed. The vaguely 'Queen Anne' dining room furniture was possibly purchased especially for this house on their marriage. Some of the more modish details and much of the bric-a-brac and flower arranging must reflect the input of the five growing daughters, but the Japonoiserie of paper umbrellas in the hearths and the shrine to Chinamania in the dining room were all features of the fashionable taste at the time the Mathers married.

1 The lobby has a standard Minton-tiled pavement and a combined coat and umbrella stand. The walls appear to be stencilled with a bold pattern on a dark ground.

2 The kitchen with the scullery beyond. The maid prepares afternoon tea. Views of the back-stairs premises of town-houses are very rare.

3 The dining room with its 'Queen Anne' suite, probably in walnut, has the conventional Turkey carpet. Other views of the room show a second piano - essential for such a musical family. The room has been made more modish by the addition of a high dado-paper. The table is set for tea but the elaborate floral centre-piece may be a survivor from a dinner party.

4 and 5 Two corners of the drawing room. The paper was probably printed in gold and the fashion for fitted carpets has passed. There are two aspidistras and the necessary equipage for afternoon tea on Mrs Mather's 'At Home' days.

6 View of one of the children's bedrooms with family pet.

1

2

3

4

5

6

THE DRAWING ROOM AT LAURENCEPARK HOUSE, STIRLINGSHIRE

This important photograph may record a decorative scheme by David Ramsay Hay, Scotland's pioneer interior decorator. A protégé of Sir Walter Scott, and inspired by the rationalist spirit of the Edinburgh Enlightenment, Hay's soubriquets include 'the first intellectual house-painter'. From 1828, with the publication of his first book, he began to apply the results of recent scientific investigation of colour theory to his trade.

In composing a scheme Hay paid great attention to a room's aspect and intended function. This light and cheerful room is far from being the standard pompous reception room of the time, and it may have been deliberately decorated to make the sunny drawing room of a 'summer residence' look crisp and cool in the sun's heat. The plain painting on the plaster panelling of the ceiling is most unusual and in a room 'of more substantial character' it would have been normal to grain this in imitation of oak.

The wooden-slat Venetians confirm a southern aspect but they were, of course, conventional protection for the costly contents of every drawing room. More unusual are the chintz curtains where a drawing room would normally have had silk.

Hay's scientific approach led to a hatred of wallpaper. In the damp Scottish climate paper became liable to 'putrefaction' and filled a room with 'the effluvia from the decayed animal and vegetable substances necessarily employed in this mode of decoration'. His solution was to oil-paint the walls and stencil them with geometric patterns in gold, which in grand houses would quote from the family heraldry. The careful spacing of the motifs here confirms that this cannot be a paper.

Hay was one of the first writers to condemn loud floral carpets. In his colour schemes even the cover of the ubiquitous centre-table had to harmonise and here it appears to be in a velvet-pile. It was probably made by Richard Whytock of Edinburgh who had first applied the technique to the manufacture of the cheap printed carpets which made his fortune. Whytock was the first carpet manufacturer to employ a full time artist-designer, winning Hay's confidence and full approval. Since Hay's schemes were founded on scientific principles he gave his decorations a hundred year life-span. This scheme was probably forty years old when it was photographed c. 1880.

THE ROUND DRAWING ROOM AT 98 GEORGE STREET, EDINBURGH

It is exceptionally rare to have such an early and comprehensive survey of a single room - dated 1858 - and one in a town house rather than a country house. However, these may have been taken as a deliberate record by its owner, the banker David Anderson of Moredun, since the house was to be purchased for Masonic Halls and its days as a family home were over. Although the photographs are Victorian, when compared with earlier documentary evidence it is clear that they also afford an insight into the appearance of Edinburgh New Town houses in the 1820s, when much of the furniture shown here must have been supplied. An unusual and individual note is struck only by the prominently displayed Old Master art collection and the grandeur of the interior architecture with its marbled columns and circular walls.

It was the practice to furnish both front and back drawing rooms in town houses en suite so that, with their connecting doors thrown open, they could function as a single unit for large parties or routs. The rooms here have identical carpets and apparently have matching wallpaper. The paper looks like an expensive flock which was standard for a room of this importance.

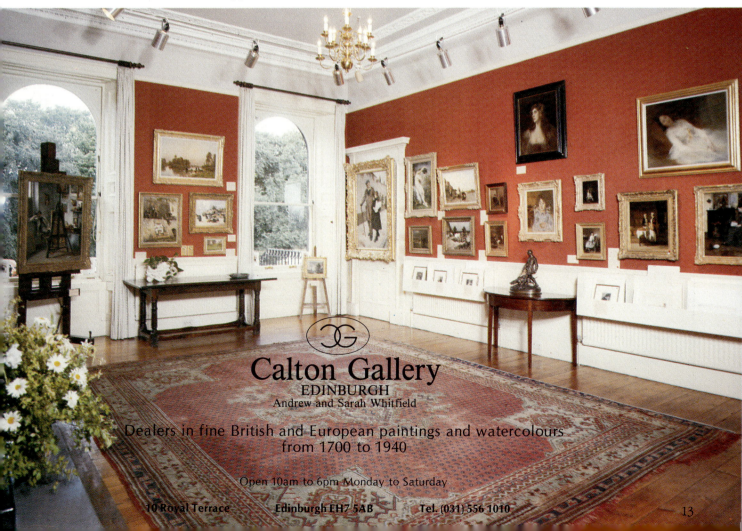

MRS FINDLAY IN HER DRAWING ROOM AT HATTON HOUSE, MIDLOTHIAN

This view of the drawing room at Hatton was taken in 1875, for inclusion in John Ritchie Findlay's privately printed history of the house. He was an important figure in Scottish life because he was proprietor of *The Scotsman*, through which he expressed his political views. Findlay merely rented the house from the Earl of Morton. This, and the fact that he used it only as a summer residence, as the lack of curtains shows, may explain why the drawing room has such old fashioned Regency furniture. The house's original contents had been dispersed by auction many years before.

Findlay employed the architect Rowand Anderson to carry out a scholarly restoration under his supervision. The decorative painting breaking up the 'vapid whitewash' of the Georgian cove, may survive from an ambitious scheme by an earlier occupant. The high gloss on the panelling is the result of the hand-burnishing of its copal varnish which seems to have been a common practice in the 1830s. The room's austerity and lack of clutter, with a plain cloth on the centre table, also reflects Findlay's own character. It was noted that the family 'lived unostentatiously' and he used his vast wealth as a public benefactor to endow the Scottish National Portrait Gallery which provided an outlet for his antiquarian interests. Although he insisted on Anderson's appointment as architect, Findlay characteristically chose to remain anonymous while the Gallery was being erected, only revealing his involvement at the opening ceremony.

THOMAS BONNAR'S DRAWING ROOM AT 7 ANN STREET, EDINBURGH

Thomas Bonnar was the head of a celebrated firm of Edinburgh decorators, founded by his father, and this room certainly displays a professional hand. It was a house in which art was worshipped. His uncle, the artist William Bonnar, was an early member of the Royal Scottish Academy. His father too had retired from the business early to devote himself to easel painting.

Bonnar himself wrote the biography of George Meikle Kemp, architect of the Scott Monument, who had married his father's sister. Many of these strands are apparent in the contents of this room. In 1879, Bonnar read a paper embodying his thoughts on decoration to the Edinburgh Architectural Association, of which he was President. It was published at their request.

His approach was romantically picturesque, and he particularly admired the richly layered look of old family houses. To provide an equivalently rich background for his own more rapidly assembled clutter he added vases and festoons to the plain Grecian cornice, and replaced the door of the press with an elaborate glazed china-cabinet in Adamesque style. The wallpapers follow the then current fashion for dividing the wall with a high dado. The simple geometric pattern of the upper paper was probably specially selected to supply an unobtrusive background to the art, and the room contains a suite of newly-made Aesthetic art-furniture, doubtless to his own design. In spite of the variety of objects, Bonnar's room has a notable repose, since each has been so carefully placed and the pictures hung with discrimination to form a balanced arrangement.

Hatton House

7 Ann Street

THE EIGHTH EARL OF STAIR'S DRAWING ROOM AND
LIBRARY AT OXENFOORD CASTLE, MIDLOTHIAN

Although these photographs date from the 1880s little
seems to have happened since 1840 when the Earl
commissioned the Edinburgh architect, William Burn, to
enlarge and modernise the castle. Burn's success as the
leading country house architect of the day derived, as
historian David Walker has shown, from his meticulous
attention to the plan, which ensured that his wealthy
aristocratic clients enjoyed luxuriously comfortable and
smooth-running houses.

Designed to cope with any domestic situation, Burn's
reception rooms inter-connect and can function as a single
unit to accommodate a large party. To this end, both rooms are
identically decorated with the same Elizabethan ceilings,
matching carpets and a crimson flock paper to show off the
gilded picture frames. Detailed scrutiny reveals however, that
this is a very unequal partnership in the drawing room's
favour. Reflecting the survival of Georgian ideals of propriety,
which dictated how different rooms ought to be furnished,
the drawing room retains the character of a state room. As the
principal reception room it attracts most of the available
funds. Burn underlines this with additional ceiling ornaments
to increase its relative expanse of gilding.

Art too is distributed on hierarchic lines. Although both
chimneypieces are of pure white statuary marble, only that in
the drawing room, with its caryatids, aspires to sculpture. The
drawing room's cabinet pictures rate as Fine Art and are
awarded more sumptuous frames than the mere portraiture
in the library. The drawing room suite is in the costly 'Louis'
revival style, with a 'gorgeous' gilded over-mantle glass to suit
the real, or equally fake, ormolu mounted antique French
cabinet furniture. If we could remove the chintz covers from
the chairs, which protected them in ordinary use, we should
find silk and rosewood frames beneath. By contrast the more
masculine library suite is in a plain and traditional Grecian
style executed in simple mahogany and robust leather.

Burn disdained the finer niceties of interior decoration.
One client was firmly told that Burn's houses were to be
finished 'with good and substantial work, and nothing else is
required.' There was no place in them for anything 'fanciful.'

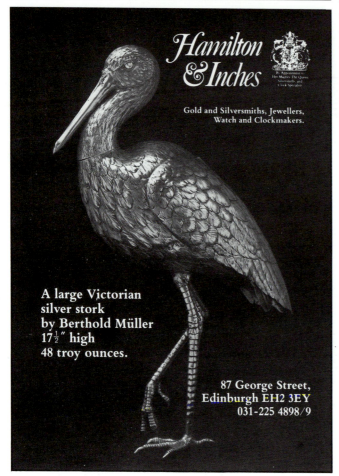
THE DRAWING ROOM OF AN UNIDENTIFIED LADY

This room, compelling in its ordinariness and frustratingly unidentified, was photographed around 1880 but fitted up forty years earlier. It has the air of being quite expensively decorated by tradesmen and is but lightly stamped with the personality of its occupant.

Although the architect supplied something severely Grecian, the upholsterer has nodded to the fashionable 'Louis look' then obligatory for drawing rooms, and introduced half-hearted rococo elements to his suite of chimney-glass, chiffonier, sofa and side-chairs. A similar restraint is notable in the standard floral fitted carpet which might almost have satisfied the criticisms of mid-century design reformers who protested at the irrationality of trampling on bouquets of flowers.

Hay would have approved of the plain oil-painted walls. Their shade is probably a deliberate contrast to the silk curtains, whose colour would have been the starting point of the scheme - crimson curtains against green walls being a favourite early Victorian scheme.

The house-painter's new-found skills in decorative painting has transformed the humble pine woodwork into a convincing imitation of satin-wood to make it worthier of a drawing-room's preciousness. To the same end the walls are trimmed with a narrow gilt fillet. The note of common sense behind much Victorian architecture ensures that a simple curtain replaces the elaborate folding-doors of the Georgian period, while the adjacent conservatory is separated by a proper window which keeps out the damp more effectively than a door. Although the owner has supplied a fine lacquer cabinet, her bric-a-brac hardly impinges on her tradesmen's creations. The sewing machine and balls of wool suggest that she might have executed the Berlin woolwork on the chair herself.

A range of photographs of Victorian interiors can be seen at the National Monuments Record, including the Scottish negatives of the London photographer, Bedford Lemere, whose ability to flatter his subjects brought him many architect clients including Charles Rennie Mackintosh. It also holds a complete set of prints by the Edinburgh photographic firm Francis Inglis & Co., which specialised in architectural subjects, and whose negatives were carelessly dispersed recently.

The finest local collection of interior photographs must be the Magnus Jackson Collection in Perth Museum, seconded only by Clapperton of Selkirk, and through their generosity, the Record has a set of the architectural views in both collections. The finest individual album is that devoted to "The Cairns", which was presented by its architect John Burnet, to his client, Mrs John P. Kitson in 1875. With her money, and perhaps too indulgent co-operation, he produced a house of such profound Gothic discomfort that it did not suggest itself for inclusion in a publication devoted to the recreation of the Victorian interior!

CREAM OF THE CAFES

Edinburgh's splendidly Victorian Café Royal came close to being destroyed in our own time. *Colin McWilliam* pays tribute to the enduring elements which make it one of the capital's most relished institutions.

Squeezed in behind the big banks of St Andrew Square, this arcaded and mansarded *bombe surprise* brought the French Second Empire to strait-laced Victorian Edinburgh and is still one of the city's most relished institutions. Yet the whole thing happened rather by chance, and in our own time was very nearly lost along with many of the best of its kind in Britain - the splendiferous Holborn Restaurant in London, for example.

The architect was Robert Paterson, who was later to design the Windsor Hotel at 100 Princes Street (now the Royal Over-Seas League) in the same vein. His client was Robert Hume, Plumber and Gasfitter, whose shop for some years was to occupy part of the ground floor (the same shape as what is

now the Crown Room immediately overhead). All the rest was opened as the New Café Royal Hotel on 8th July 1863, by Mr Grieve who already owned the North British Hotel and the old Café Royal in West Register Street, as they then existed. The ground and first floors provided, in the words of *The Scotsman,* "the Great Dining House of the Metropolis", served by kitchens in the basement, while in the upper floors were "numerous cheerful sitting-rooms and well-ventilated bedrooms". These, with their names from Burns and Scott, still survive upstairs but are frequented only by the ghosts of Victorian guests.

The Circle Bar was formed in 1893 by a different architect, A.N. Macnaughtan. He removed the longitudinal

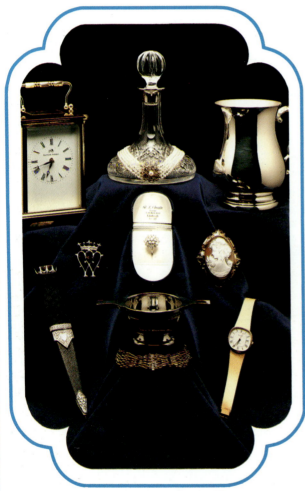

22

wall of Hume's old shop, and replaced it with rolled steel beams (concealed by plasterwork) and a massive iron pillar, like a French Gothic tree. Originally a Smoking Room, in 1893 it became yet another restaurant and in 1900 J. Macintyre Henry installed the octagonal bar, the great mahogany chimneypiece and the six tile pictures by Doulton of Lambeth. These had been shown at the South Kensington Exhibition of Inventions and Music in 1885, and now edified the diners with their portrayal of six great discoveries; three in the field of printing (William Caxton's movable type, Benjamin Franklin's broadsheets, Robert Peel's patterns on calico), two in steam power (Watt and Stephenson), and one in photography (Niepce and Daguerre). The artists were J. Eyre, K. Sturgeon and W. Nunn. Today's horseshoe-shaped wall-seats correspond with Henry's design, but the rather lightweight gantry in the middle of the island bar is of recent date.

The Oyster Bar's corner entrance with its undulating pediment was inserted in 1898, and the interior much as we know it today was in existence by 1900, Charles Clark being the owner and Henry once again the architect. Under an earlier ceiling with 'Jacobean' ribs, Irish harp and Scots thistle, this beautiful room takes you back to the last proud days of the Victorian era and the confident threshold of the Edwardian. To the former belong two more Doulton pictures in which, as historian Alistair Rowan described them in *Country Life,* "the first Cunarder Umbria and a Liverpool paddle boat steam perpetually across the glistening surfaces"; they were painted by Esther Lewis, and may first have been seen at the Edinburgh 1886 Exhibition. So do the stained glass windows specially made by the prolific Edinburgh firm of Ballantine & Gardiner, of six British sportsmen including a member of The Royal Company of Archers, (the Queen's Bodyguard in Scotland) with longbow, and a strikingly similar

modern marksman with shotgun - the muzzle and obediently closed eyes of the Monarch of the Glen lying at his feet. To the latter era, a perfect foil to this rich Victorian colour, belong the warm mahogany of Henry's mirrored screens with their eclectic carving, the liver-coloured marble bar and the black-and-white marble floor. Only the wavering brilliance of gaslight is missing from this durable ensemble.

From 1908 to 1946 the Register Commercial Temperance Hotel occupied, rather surprisingly, the upper floors. Meantime Charles Clark's son, Charles Venus Clark, wrestled with the perennial Edinburgh problem of ground-floor profit versus first-floor access and finally decided on the first, returning everything in 1926 to the status quo. Eglinton Hotels re-opened the sumptuous Crown Room on the first floor in 1946, thus inaugurating the golden age of the ten shilling lunch and £2 dinner which is still fondly remembered today.

Like many good things this had an end – but not so the Café Royal itself, thanks to a combination of private protest and public control. Grand Metropolitan Hotels took over in 1965, and four years later agreed to sell out to Woolworths of Princes Street who wanted the site for a car park. Only the City Planning Officer, Tom Hewitson, stood in the way, and aided by a petition with 8700 signatures he decided that the great interior merit of the building, which was listed, justified the refusal of planning consent. His committee agreed, and Scotland has reason to be grateful. Listed Building Control of interior character was from thenceforth acknowledged. On the Friday evening of their decision one of the signatories, the then Earl of Dalkeith, was seen at his private celebration dinner at the Café Royal on his way home from Westminster. Since then, Woolworths has disappeared from Princes Street. The Café Royal is still ours to enjoy.

The Oyster Bar (preceding page) is owned by Brian Donkin and the Circle Bar (above) by Coronation Inns, Ltd.

MOUNT STUART

The greatest patron of architecture in Victorian times was a Scotsman. *Nic Allen* visits the magnificent island home built by the 3rd Marquess of Bute at Mount Stuart, which is still the family home.

Groups of wallabies once grazed in the policies of Mount Stuart. Now that they have gone the surroundings give nothing away. Quite, well tended fields and woodlands exude dignified, conservative, landed wealth and suggest that at the centre of the estate there is a home to match: a fastidious, if slightly portly, Palladian mansion, perhaps, or a neo-baronial pile? Not a bit of it. Set in the gentle parkland which slopes down to the Firth of Clyde is a vast, hollow cube of a building, covering almost an acre and with a space at its heart which quite takes the breath away.

To obtain some ideas of the Great Hall of Mount Stuart, walk into the Scottish National Portrait Gallery in Edinburgh, designed by the same architect some five years later. The Gallery's central hall is impressive enough. Two tiers of sandstone arcading rise to a flat, star speckled ceiling. Now increase its height by a third, turn the stone columns into marble of half a dozen colours – reds, greens, greys – and bathe them in the light of half a dozen more, filtering through vast stained glass panels. Roof this with a great celestial dome twinkling with stars and alive with giant, ghostly-white, Zodiacal figures and you have an impression of the Great Hall of Mount Stuart. This is no genteel

Above: The stained glass panels behind Lord Bute and above the entrance door display the arms of the three earldoms of Bute - Bute, Dumfries, and Windsor.

Opposite page: "No attempt to underwhelm here", one visitor is said to have remarked on entering the Great Hall.

Previous page: Looking down into the Great Hall.

Opposite: *Private worship on a public scale: the design of the chapel's lantern was based on the Cathedral at Zaragoza.*

Below: *'The Lord of the Hunt' took a decade to weave, and was one of two huge tapestries commissioned from the Edinburgh Tapestry Company by the 4th Marquess to decorate the Great Hall.*

country seat, the hotch-potch accumulation of centuries. It is the palazzo of some great merchant prince and the single-minded realisation of a personal fantasy.

But there is no wilful deception in the seeming contradictions between Mount Stuart and its surroundings – rather, a true reflection of the background of its creator, John Patrick Crichton-Stuart, 3rd Marquess of Bute. Here was a man who could trace back his family's territorial dominance of the Island of Bute for five centuries, yet owed the greater part of his fortune to the Industrial Revolution. At the tiny Welsh port of Cardiff, recently brought into the family by marriage, his father had created vast docks which, by the middle of the nineteenth century, were exporting more coal than any others in the world. "What will he do with it?" asked the newspapers in 1868, when the 3rd Marquess came of age and gained control of his fortune.

The answer was that, in the great age of the gentleman amateur, Bute chose to use his wealth and his remarkable mind to become the greatest of them all in terms of both his range of interests and his depth of knowledge of each. In his relatively short life he was to build, rebuild or restore a score of houses; to master, it was said, twenty-one languages; to spend ten years translating the Roman Breviary; to become the co-author of a book on psychic phenomena and the patron of countless causes, from the development of the Scottish Universities to the advancement of Jewish interests. "I believe Lord Bute would be interested in these", remarked a friend to the custodian of some dwarf Japanese trees. "Yes", replied the custodian, "his Lordship knows a lot about plants. But then he knows a lot about most things, don't he sir?"

Mount Stuart became the expression of many of these passionate interests. When the main part of the early eighteenth century house burned down in 1879 Bute commissioned, as architect for the rebuilding, not his old architectural crony William Burges, designer of Bute's Glamorganshire neo-medieval fantasies of Cardiff Castle and Castell Coch, but Robert Rowand Anderson. In the Welsh houses, it can be difficult to distinguish where Burges's influence ends and Bute's begins. At Mount Stuart matters are clearer: it is Bute's multifarious passions which are revealed, one by one, as the visitor passes through the interior.

Heraldry was one such passion and, even as you come into the house, this becomes apparent from the stained glass panels above the entrance bearing the arms of the Marquess's three earldoms. A short flight of stairs brings the visitor into the Great Hall and no sooner have you grown accustomed to its dark, multi-coloured magnificence than Mount Stuart springs another surprise. A door leads into the chapel and suddenly all is light and gleaming, towering white marble, tempered only by the blood-red glow from the stained glass high in the lantern. It is a fitting tribute to a constant religious questing which took the young Bute into the Catholic church.

Conversion to Catholicism, however, presented no obstacle to a continuing interest in psychic research and astrology. The latter interest is to be seen not only in the ceiling on the Great Hall, but more intimately and directly, in the Marquess's horoscope room on the second floor of Mount Stuart. Here the night sky of the day of his birth illuminates the ceiling. It could so easily seem to be a piece of monumental hubris, but somehow it expresses instead an almost childlike fascination with the subject and a straightforward delight in the ability to turn fantasy into reality. The blue of the sky set in a sea of unfaded gilt and red dazzles the

Opposite page: A gilded ceiling, the background for exotic African birds, surrounds the representation of the night sky on the day of the 3rd Marquess's birth.

visitor with its brightness and simplicity. Here is Burges's neo-medieval influence on Bute at its strongest; a love of splendid but pure and unadulterated craftsmanship and use of materials; a rejection of any form of decorative deception. The same rules are applied to both architectural decoration and furnishings. The furniture beneath the celestial ceiling is splendidly crafted and finely inlaid in mother of pearl, but it is massive and honest, with no attempt to hide the nature of the wood. Bute had taken on board Burges's disdain for Georgian veneers and Regency daintiness.

The influence of Burges and the Welsh building schemes is also apparent in the craftsmen chosen to work at Mount Stuart. Rowand Anderson chose a Glasgow firm, Watt & Wilson, as builders, but firms such as Campbell, Smith & Campbell, who were responsible for the decorative work, and artists such as W.F. Lonsdale, who both designed stained glass and painted friezes, were old established Bute favourites from Cardiff Castle.

One obvious irony bounces back and forward through the story of Mount Stuart. Here was a monument to pre-industrial values built from the proceeds of an industrial fortune. Here also was a building which, for all its trumpeting of medieval decorative simplicities, also contained the very latest in the technologies of convenience. Anderson made sure that hot water pipes throughout the building provided central heating, electric light shone from hundreds of mosque lamps, the very latest in plumbing systems were "executed in the English style of workmanship" and the house was serviced by a new waterworks built on the moors two miles above Mount Stuart.

But the house remained unfinished. Bute was "never out of the mortar tub", Rowand Anderson remarked resignedly. "Why not let it be finished, and off your mind?" he once begged his great patron.

"But why should I hurry over what is my chief pleasure?" Bute replied. True to his word, he left work to be done on every one of his houses when he died in 1900. But there are good reasons to be grateful for this. The incentive to add the final touches to these great schemes seems to have contributed, at least in part, to a remarkable continuity of interest in their architectural and decorative culture among the 3rd Marquess's descendants.

His son, for instance, effectively brought the Edinburgh Tapestry company into being to create two great tapestries to hang in the Great Hall. The interests of his great-grandson, the 6th and present Marquess, encompass areas of the decorative arts as wide-ranging as textile weaving and woodworking. There are signs of continuing activity everywhere at Mount Stuart: scaffolding on the north face of the main building, cartoons in situ of a frieze intended to decorate a ground floor room, newly completed joinery work in the magnificent second-floor conservatory.

Lord Bute ponders the right material to use on the screens between the columns on the main staircase. He winces at the sight of the starkly painted walls beneath the nativity ceiling. He explains that he intends to extend the line and colours of the ceiling down on to the walls. It will look magnificent. "Take a photograph of it when it is finished in two years' time", he says. It is an irresistible invitation to follow to completion in the 1980s a remarkable monument to a remarkable Victorian.

*The second-floor conservatory (**opposite**) with its view of the steeple of the chapel, is now nearing completion.*

*Medieval fantasy meets Victorian technology (**below**): between the marble arches and the leaded windows is to be found the most up-to-date plumbing that the 1880s could provide.*

ARCHETYPAL AYTON

Ayton Castle in Berwickshire is the most prominent of Scottish country houses. Viewed from the east coast Edinburgh to London railway line which cuts a swathe across the 5000 acre estate, it is a spectacular sight admired every day by countless British Rail passengers. As *Sheila Mackay* discovered, even visitors approaching by road are struck by Ayton's dominance of the landscape, in the way that pilgrims approaching a medieval abbey must have been.

The straightforward Scottish Baronial exterior of Ayton Castle offers no clues to its lavish interiors.

Ayton's first owner, W. Mitchell-Innes, a director of a Scottish Bank, was keen to evoke exactly that impression, as was his architect, James Gillespie Graham, who finished building Ayton in 1846. From its lofty hilltop site, this Victorian gentleman's dream of a country house commands views of fine rolling Border countryside, its dignified sandstone towers signalling wealth and authority.

The reality of today, however, is less romantic for Ayton's hard-working owner, David Liddell-Grainger. He takes a maxim something he frequently says: "If you must restore, go the whole hog", and has set himself the task of perfecting the intentions of Gillespie Graham and Mitchell-Innes who both died before the interiors were completed. As an example, he is working on a scheme for the unfurnished all-white ceiling in the drawing room. With the help of the Stenhouse Conservation Centre in Edinburgh, its ornate plasterwork is soon to be painted in what has been discovered to be the original scheme. In an upstairs bedroom, also white, a little sampler of how this too should be, has been painted on a wall and cornice. There is also work to be done to re-instate original features obliterated by previous owners. A case in point is the intriguing patch of marble-work on a column otherwise painted white all over, announcing hidden splendour soon to be uncovered.

Not that the restoration work is just beginning. David Liddell-Grainger has been hard at it for years. The library, once painted red by his own ancestors (who purchased Ayton from Mitchell-Innes's son in 1888) is now as it should be. A handsome, tasteful room, rich and inviting, its warm orange-brown walls are cooled and graced by an ornate light-olive and gold ceiling. This room is to be found at the end of the elegant hall, which was hand-painted in 1872 by the Edinburgh firm of Bonnar & Carfrae in a tracery of stylised flowers, including the thistle and the rose. The stencil-work is as good as new and David Liddell-Grainger has restored the rich ochre marbled pillars which announce the entrance hall —

Huge sheets of undivided plate glass were proudly installed in many country houses from the 1850s. The elegant examples shown above and opposite, shed sunlight on the informal writing desk at the end of the hall, while the family's Labradors dream of an afternoon excursion.

entered directly from the front door, as was the custom in the Middle Ages.

Although Mitchell-Innes never lived in the house he left his mark on the place in a pious quasi-heraldic inscription carved over the front door and painted on the ceiling of the entrance hall. Inscriptions and homilies executed in carving, paint and embroidery were a Victorian speciality. 'Except the Lord Build a House They Labour in Vain that Build It' and 'Home Sweet Home' were favourites. Just over the Scottish Border at Cragside, Lord Armstrong, the millionaire arms dealer, had 'East or West Home is Best' inscribed on a fireplace, while at Ayton the nouveau riche Mitchell-Innes fulsomely announ-

ced himself to be favoured by God in the motto he chose: *Deo Favente*.

The truth is that his fortune hinged far less on God's favour than that of Miss Innes, an Edinburgh heiress whom he married when still a humble bank clerk. He rose swiftly to become a director of a prominent Scottish bank, embezzling her trust funds until beneficiaries rumbled him to the Edinburgh newspaper, *The Thistle*. Mitchell-Innes bought up the paper in an unsuccessful attempt to silence a scandal which eventually drove him to suicide. When he was buried in Ayton cemetery, he had built houses at Ingliston and Stowe, as well as the nearly-finished Ayton Castle.

Ayton's interiors display that

peculiar mix of grandly formal and domestic rooms so beloved of Victorian country house owners. There are also some surprises. Take the absence of a staircase leading up from the hall, for example. Grand staircases leading to grand halls were generally favoured, not least by ladies of the house who might sweep down, proffering a preview of their finery to guests assembled below. Ayton has a modest entrance hall and the main staircase is hidden from view. It is a turnpike or spiral stair, a classic feature of the Border keep and renaissance tower house of Scotland. If Gillespie Graham selected that form for aesthetic reasons, it must also have appealed at a more practical level. An internal stair, snug against the

winds that often blow on Ayton's hilltop, is a welcome route up to the corridors and bedrooms above, even today.

The small dining room off the hall, where Ayton's Victorian owners presided over formal afternoon tea, is an 1860s extension by David Bryce of Gillespie Graham's plan. Although there were other plans in the next two decades – to add a ballroom, for example – the only other Bryce addition was to the formal dining room window. From here, guests replete with wine and good food might step out to admire from three sides the rich farmland of the Ayton estate and, on the horizon to the west, the perimeter of Hutton Castle estate, owned by the collector William Burrell, a

neighbour of David Liddell-Grainger's grandparents. The marvellous ceiling in this room has already been painted to bring out its originally intended glory and, to add to the room's grandeur, appropriate curtains are now being selected with guidance from the Victoria and Albert Museum.

David Liddell-Grainger enjoys speculating about the reactions of the Victorian owners of Ayton if they re-visited today. They would surely frown at the entrance hall's delightful clutter of things out of place — country hats, riding hats, sunhats, family photographs, a table festooned with books and papers, a piano which someone is learning to play. The grand master bedroom is now the boudoir for

Formality and informality meet in the entrance hall. This corner (left) shows the fine hand painted wall decoration by Bonnar & Carfrae of Edinburgh, one of the recently restored marbled arches - and the Labradors, now ready for a walk. The boudoir (above) was the master bedroom in Gillespie Graham's plan. Elaborate plasterwork decoration is an unusual feature on doors, window frames and furniture rail. Festoon blinds, made up in a traditional print by Remus of Edinburgh, emphasise the feminine character of the room.

relaxing in the evening, the kitchen has been converted to manageable proportions, and a private dining room was built in the 1960s within an unwanted grander room. But most of all he relishes the reaction they might have to changes in the servant's kitchen, now given over to local Scout groups who store tents and other equipment here and camp out in the grounds.

Over a century ago thirty people sat down to eat five meals every day in the servant's kitchen. Ayton was a grand house run by forty servants, including laundry, garden and stable staff, ruled over by the housekeeper and the butler. It took a fleet of servants to maintain the central heating system which pushed hot air through the corridors, and the coal fires and candles in the rooms, as well as the fetching and carrying of water before the house was plumbed later in the century. For that event one of the towers was

put to use to contain a water tank of 650 gallons capacity, supplied from a nearby hill as it still is today.

Astonishingly enough, the interiors of Ayton Castle are nowadays managed by only two part-time local women armed, of course, with the latest technology of which the vacuum cleaner is still the most revolutionary invention of all housework aids. And each year David Liddell-Grainger, a descendant of Richard Grainger, the Newcastle developer dubbed 'the Cubbitt of the North', plans the greater works — exteriors in the summer, interiors in the winter. His family motto is centuries old, straighforward and, unlike that of the unfortunate Mitchell-Innes, free from false piety: *Valour is stronger than a battering ram*. It is represented throughout the house in rams' heads carved on furniture and even moulded on the ends of brass curtain rails. It serves his painstaking dedication to Ayton well.

Previous page: The library is very much as it was intended to be over a century ago - a pleasant, gentleman's sitting room. However, the child's toys on the ottoman give a hint that this room, with its piles of magazines, books, family photographs, drinks tray and enormous log basket, is enjoyed by everyone in the house. The elaborate gilded ceiling and the walls have been restored to their original colouring. Leather bound volumes include 'Letters of Queen Victoria', 'Scott's Poetical Works', 'Salmon Rivers of Scotland', 'Berwickshire Naturalist', and the 'Waverley Novels'. Local craftsmen helped to build Ayton Castle in 1846 and maintain it today. The electrician from Duns (opposite) has been re-wiring part of the house. Above left: The view from the spiral staircase up to the ceiling-rose where paint scrapes - see detail of marbled pillar, above right - reveal restoration work soon to be tackled.

42

CARDY
INSIDE OUT

This peaceful retreat in Fife was created by the
descendants of Alexander Selkirk, the famous castaway
upon whom Daniel Defoe based the character of
Robinson Crusoe. House and contents have changed
little in over a century as *Jeremey Bruce-Watt* discovered.

Classical statues cast in concrete and a 'Louis revival' garden seat,
well-placed to overlook fine sea views, grace the approach. The bronze
bust of Alexander Selkirk by T. Stuart Burnett was commissioned by
Cardy House's first owner.

The directions for a visit to Cardy House are simple: "It's the last house in the village, up on the hill to the left." No more is needed. The village is Lower Largo, a pleasing straggle of colour-washed buildings, mainly eighteenth century weavers' and fishermens' houses, set on the shore of the Firth of Forth in the charming corner of Fife known as the East Neuk.

The house is a mansion compared with the neighbouring cottages and crow-stepped, pantiled tenements. Shrouded in tall sycamores it seems to hold itself aloof from the way the world has gone.

This is surely one of the most evocative homes in Scotland, lived in by several generations of the same remarkable family, and to visit it is to step back into an age quite lost and gone — but yet not entirely, for at Cardy House the Victorian era is perpetuated with an unusal awareness, sense of values, and loving care.

The heavy wrought iron gate is the original, painted white. At the end of the short drive overshadowed by laburnums visitors are met by a grey stone sculpture of an Arcadian youth draped in a feline fur. The square grey house has a crouching lion at each gable and, above the door, a statue of Altas supports the world. Shells from the beach lie scattered at the door, and from the terrace the view is of the East Lothian coast across the Firth, Inchkeith island far to the west, the Bass Rock to the east.

The house itself dates from 1871. It has been furnished, decorated, owned and occupied by members of one family, but what is so unusual for a house of this kind is that almost everything the first residents knew is still in its appointed place. The family name is Gillies, latterly Jardine, and these are the direct decendants of Alexander Selkirk, the celebrated sailor, pirate and castaway whose adventures inspired Daniel Defoe to write *Robinson Crusoe*. His

humble thatched house stood in Lower Largo's main street. Today the bronze statue of Selkirk in his castaway's clothes stands on the site, attracting visitors from all over the world.

Cardy House was the work of David Selkirk Gillies, a great-great-great grandson, born in 1843. He left the village school at 13, and despite little formal education, his drive and business acumen led him, when only twenty-four, to open a fishing net factory, employing sixty of the local women. Orders came from as far afield as Australia. A portrait photograph shows David Gillies aged forty-two — with high domed forehead, thinning hair but dashing Dundreary whiskers. A philanthropist and visionary, this remarkable man acted as legal advisor to the people of Lower Largo, and compiled and preserved the records of the community.

Half way up the red pine staircase which ascends from the front door of Cardy House, the visitor comes face to face with Alexander Selkirk in his goatskins — a huge sombre bust, the only one cast from the statue at the birthplace. On either side are eighteenth century liquor bottles found under floorboards in the village — a large green globe for brandy and a dark, flat-sided flask for rum, made that way for easy loading into smugglers' boats.

The landing is a fantastic study in sepia: dark wooden banisters, dark panelling, an immense wooden chest, Victorian paintings closely hung on hand decorated walls. A paraffin lamp with the white globe lit to show the family to bed still stands in the bracket fixed to the banister rail. On the chest stands a musical box, and Victorian plants sprout from Victorian china pots in Victorian plantholders.

In the drawing room, off the landing, there is little of twentieth century origin either in the room or in the view from the large bay window. There is a sensation

of the years having gently passed, and still passing, but at the same time standing still. The four foot long brass telescope on the table shows the East Lothian coast in sharp relief, and the moon in vivid detail. Two huge mirrors are encased in elaborate gilt frames incorporating cameos of Queen Victoria as a young woman. Three generations of the Gillies family stare out from daguerreo types framed in red velvet and gilt, flanked by two ebony elephants with ivory tusks and toenails and shining eyes. The violins made by two musical brothers, William and Robert — who in the 1880s designed, built and raced their yachts named *Quaver* and *Semiquaver* — still stand in the corner. A little table is inlaid with the patterns for draughts and bezique.

Many of the paintings in their heavy gilt frames are by Scottish artists of the last century, who called at the house and left them as presents, or in lieu of payment for some business transaction with David Gillies. The doors have kept their porcelain handles and fingerplates. The house bells, pulled by hand, still ring in the kitchen below, and although no one is there to answer, their leisurely jangle is like an echo from a bygone age.

The ambience here is quite different from that in grand houses whose formal displays may be magnificent, but whose rooms, because they are not lived in, inevitably feel impersonal and cold. Everywhere in Cardy House one is aware of a gentle, brooding homeliness. Half close the eyes and look round at the empty chairs and it is easy to imagine them occupied by earlier kith and kin. Their names in copperplate are on the flyleaves of open books. A sampler with a text and the embroidered inscription: *Christina Tait, aged 12, 1885,* lies on a chair, as though the little girl had just laid it down and gone out of the room, which in a way she has.

1

2

3

4

The present chatelaine of Cardy House is Ivy Jardine, now widowed, whose two sons are the ninth generation to follow Alexander Selkirk in direct descent. One of her multitudinous ploys has been to trace the family back to 1657 — not such a difficult exercise, since most of the relevant papers lay in Cardy's library of 200-year-old books or in the drawers of writing desks.

Anything and everything to do with Scotland interests her, and there are few aspects of the national life and culture that she does not know something about. After she met her husband Allan (Thomas Allan Jardine) she took to lecturing on local history, holding keep-fit classes, organising exhibitions, writing and publishing a history of Lower Largo, copiously illustrated with photographs from Cardy House. A second book is about Selkirk's island of Juan Fernandez, which she has visited.

At the death of James Gillies, the son of David who built the house, Cardy came to Allan and Ivy, with all its treasures and family mementoes. Where many a less sensitive family would have set about destroying it, they allowed it to remain, apart from essential modernisation, exactly as it was. Allan died in 1986. In Ivy's passport her occupation is given as "Housewife". "I think", she says, "a more accurate description would be 'Mistress of Cardy House'!".

Most of the ground floor dining room is taken up by the vast mahogany table. David Gillies, the Earl and Countess of Aberdeen and their guests sat here on the day in 1885 the statue of Alexander Selkirk, commissioned by David, was unveiled. A long Chesterfield couch with button-backed leather upholstery occupies the corner by the window. There is a writing desk topped by a glass-fronted cabinet full of glasses. The big sideboard is embellished with a carved bird of prey. A glass case contains a century old set of silver-mounted bagpipes once belonging to a man called Grant — Ivy Jardine's maiden name. The fire-irons are the ones ordered for the house by David Selkirk Gillies. Sun streams through the window and everything glows, glitters or sparkles — brass and glass, polished timber and delicate gilt, marble and fine panelling. Like all the rooms in Cardy, it looks and feels lived in, which, of course, it is.

Perhaps the most evocative place in the house is the main bedroom on the upper floor, across the landing from the drawing room. The high Scottish double bed has a headpiece pointed like a church window and the snow white damask bedspread bears a woven motif: Cardy House, Largo, the initials D.G. and I.G., and the date 1889. (David and Isabella, the first householders, were married in 1886.)

The dressing table displays an array of Victorian bottles and phials for perfumes and creams and attar of roses, and the green and white ewer and basin on the white-topped marble washstand are as fresh-looking as when they where first placed there. The fireplace has a black marble surround and an ornamental cast iron grate, with a small circular hob for heating the early and late kettles. Beside it is the vast rosewood wardrobe, with individually designed compartments for husband and wife, which had to be imported in sections and assembled by the local joiners. Photographs on the wall show David Gillies and his equally remarkable brother James, known as "James the Whaler" who spent years at sea as a ship's carpenter — a jolly man in a seafarer's hat, with twinkling eyes and a fluffy fringe of beard.

From the bedroom window there is a fine view of the sea and the formal Victorian garden below. A subterranean passage leads from the house under a narrow footpath to the garden where large ornamental urns

Previous page: Ivy Jardine often entertains friends for tea at the massive mahogany dining room table with its deeply-buttoned leather chairs and characteristic Turkey carpet. Her enthusiasm for Cardy House has helped to preserve the splendour and atmosphere of how things once were.

1 The landing - a fantastic study in sepia, enriched with the wall painting which occurs throughout the house. This was a later decorative overlay of the original scheme, executed by James Darling of Edinburgh, a family friend.

2 The dining room with a detail, 3 of the highly polished black marble chimneypiece and gilded overmantle. The splendid original 'garniture', consisting of a heavy clock, a pair of Bohemian glass vases and a pair of theatrical bronzes, has attracted a pair of Indian elephants. The bell-pulls and clock match the chimneypiece.

4 Detail of James Darling's later wall painting which suggests a strong interest in early Scottish painted decoration.

Nothing but the best would do for the drawing room dedicated to the arts (opposite), where elaborate gilding survives in the ornamental ceiling and frieze and massive curtain rails and picture rods finished with white porcelain and gilt knobs to match the bell-pulls. A conventional Adam-revival marble chimneypiece supports one of a pair of overmantle mirrors which, with the tapestry curtains, may belong to the second phase of redecoration of the house (around 1890) which included James Darling's wall paintings.

1 A corner of the drawing room dominated by the exotically veneered and gilded upright piano by Paterson & Sons, Edinburgh, with a pair of ostrich eggs and grandly gilded framed landscape paintings hung with chains from the original sturdy rod.

2 Brass telescope in the bay window which commands spectacular sea views. Holland blinds edged with lace protect the drawing room contents from the full glare of the sun.

3 and 4 Boxes collected by several generations include a Georgian knife box, locked tea caddy and 'apprentice boxes' made by members of the Gillies family.

5 A marble topped wash stand in the bedroom holds the neccessities of a pre-plumbing age, from the chamber pot to coloured glass bottle containing eau de Cologne.

overflow with nasturtiums, and lifesize grey stone figures of nymphs and shepherds continue their century-long watch. The birds sing louder than the sound of the sea, and nothing else is heard. There is a curious feeling of expectancy as though people may be about to enter from the shadows, like actors on to a stage.

Much of the open space is taken up by the large lawn laid out by David Gillies for use as a bowling green by the women working in the net factory. In one corner is a little alcove with slatted benches where they sat during breaks. Here and there are white ornamental garden seats, just where they were in the 1880s, according to photographs of the family taken at that time. Flowering plumes of pampas grass wave above a scattering of white and yellow tea roses and a thick rank of sweet peas. A heavy grass roller rests in its parking place in a corner. A nymph with a stone smile offers a wreath of flowers.

The eastern boundary is formed by the red brick wall of David Gillies's net factory, with its grey slate roof, large skylights – and contents intact from the day it closed in 1886. Through a window is glimpsed a huge Dickensian clerk's desk, with a date card showing 22 September. At the works entrance, an almost naked cherub has surrendered an arm and a forearm to the ravages of time, and on the other side his companion has all but vanished, leaving only a tiny pair of naked feet still in situ.

A low-flying warplane thunders above the deserted beach and the pantiled roofs of the sleepy village, and suddenly the ugly din of modern times shatters the enduring peace. In seconds it has gone, leaving Cardy House with its Saltire flying from the tall flagpole on the roof, the naval signal mast at the foot of the garden, and all the beautiful things which have graced the house for a hundred unchanging years.

Two of the classical statues in concrete which survive, only a little the worse for a century's weathering. The Pompeian youth, appropriately clad, reposes in the once formal garden while Atlas, poised above the entrance porch, bears the world aloft.

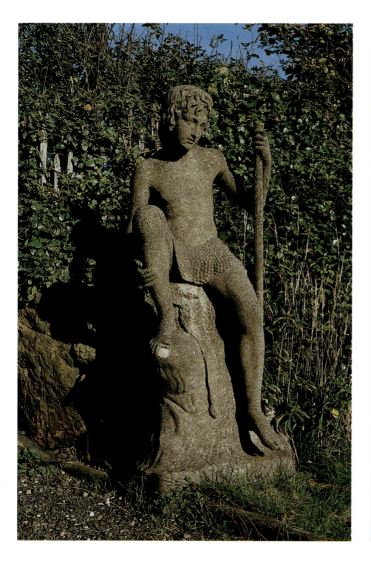

DONALD'S BALMORAL

Most of Scotland's thatched croft houses have been abandoned to sheep and the elements but Donald Mackenzie takes pride in the fact that his house is Grade A listed like Balmoral Castle. It is full of treasured memories — and almost wind and watertight. *Sheila Mackay* paid him a visit.

Number 12, Lower Ardelve, awaits the removal of its plastic 'hairnet' and the welcome new thatch of reeds cut by Jim Souness of Cairdean nan Taighean Tugha (Friends of the Thatched Houses) from the croft's field. Bundles at the porch entrance will be stacked, with others, to dry out.

Donald Mackenzie sits beside the hanging lum of the croft house at No. 12 Lower Ardelve as his father did and his father's father before that. If you consider that Donald Mackenzie's father was born in 1856, that is going back a bit.

No one can be sure when the house was built. Perhaps it was not quite as early as the two coins bearing the head of George III which hang in the parlour indicate. Mounted on a piece of varnished wood from Donald Mackenzie's boat, an inscription reads; "1812: Tokens for lodgings given in Glasgow to men from the Highlands who came to give their labour in the Industrial Revolution and leave their mark in shipbuilding and engineering that exist to this day".

What is certain is that for a century-and-a-half the seasons have come and gone, winter to spring, spring to summer, and summer to those glorious autumns which turn the hills of Kintail aglow with golden brown ferns, soft purple heather and entwine the croft house in a profusion of red rowan and honeysuckle berries.

*The parlour dresser (**opposite**) overflows. Treasured memories contained in its delightful clutter of plates and jugs spill over onto adjoining shelves (**above**) where a Toby-jug shares space with special china, including a set of cups and saucers commemorating the Coronation of George VI.*

Season after season the house itself has resisted the changes which time has impressed on other croft houses on mainland Scotland, leaving Donald Mackenzie's the only thoroughbred – a fact made final in 1974 when an official preservation order dropped through his door stating that his home was now a Grade A listed building. Thus, just as he might have been getting around to making a few changes, fate decreed otherwise.

The present owner of No. 12 Lower Ardelve was given the same name as his father, Donald Mackenzie, who married Isabella Macrae, daughter of Donald Macrae of Camas-luinie. Their portraits hang in the bedroom beside that of The Rev. Dr. Angus Galbraith, Free Church Minister of Lochalsh. It is as if, grouped together, their collective image still exerts an influence to keep things as they always were.

From his rightful place by the parlour fire, Donald Mackenzie conjures up memories and stories of the crofting days which are over now that he is past eighty; though to exercise his arthritic knees he still happily rides a bicycle.

A single chimney would once have sent smoke up through a central hole in the roof. That was before two fireplaces with wooden chimneys were constructed in each gable end of the house. Wood is burned now, not the peat which Donald remembers being set, damp blocks to the back of the fire, dry to the front, under the all-purpose Dutch oven which his mother used to bake in. He demonstrates with his hands how she lifted hot ashes onto its lid to cook the top of rounds of scones. She produced slow-simmering soups and stews too, though herring and potatoes were the mainstay of the family's diet.

Cooking nowadays is on a Calor gas stove, a fact which evokes a story Donald Mackenzie relishes, recalling a time in the 1950s when the "Hydro Board" was inciting crofters like him to convert to electricity. "They sent a photographer down and got two villagers to dress up as removal men, and snapped them carrying in a brand-new cooker as if it were for us. They got as far as the door, took the snap and then they carried the cooker back to their van. My niece joked about grabbing the stove off them and locking it inside. But, unfortunately, that was the last we heard of the stove – until I went to the Highland Show at Inverness. There was that photograph all over the place, and us still with the Calor gas. It was just propaganda!"

Donald was one of five children brought up in the two rooms which formed the family's typical croft house. His parents slept in a box bed, pulled down at night, placed between the window and the fireplace. A corrugated iron porch was added later to contain a stone sink. The front windows look directly over Loch Duich with fine views of Eilean Donan Castle which Donald recalls being rebuilt when he was a boy, around 1913. One tiny window to the back gives a peep out of the closet to the hills.

In the parlour are four chairs, a table, the fireplace, two presses and a dresser crowded with plates, a fine row of jugs, and curious objects like thistle-shaped cruets and a container in the form of a corn-on-the-cob, perhaps brought back from the New World in the last century. Donald remembers an itinerant tinker making a new metal handle to replace the broken china one.

In the bedroom: a wooden trunk, a bed, portraits and paintings, two chests-of-drawers bearing memorabilia including a black homburg in mint condition for church-going, a wash jug and basin, a Victorian fireplace decorated with simple striped tiles, an open cupboard. And on the bedside table with the Vicks Menthol Rub, a Gaelic Bible, some Free Church magazines, other books in Gaelic, the writings of

Opposite page: 1 Portraits of Donald Mackenzie's parents hang above the bed.
2 The chest of drawers is a respository for prints, pictures, wash jug and basin and church-going homburg. Nineteenth century patterned linoleum, with a Chinese motif, covers the floor.
3 A romantic print of a scene from 'Young Lochinvar' above the characteristic fireplace with its simple, strongly-coloured tiles and brass hood.

1

2

3

Descartes.

This, Donald's bedroom, is where the children slept in the days when the croft land behind the house contained crops and vegetables in season, ducks, hens, a few cows, a horse and a pony whose important task was to carry down the peats, which the whole family once went to cut from peat banks on the hills five miles away.

They fished too, for saith, ling, cod and herring which they salt-cured, some for themselves and some for others, selling half-a-barrel containing several hundred fish to families in the hills. Each year, to enrich the croft land, rafts of seaweed were towed in to the shores of the loch and set in piles to be rainwashed for fertiliser.

There are few thatched croft houses like Donald Mackenzie's left now, and he is justly proud of

it, pointing out that, in its own way, it is as important as the sovereign's Scottish residence at Balmoral. Not that he has had much help from "the authorities" who listed it and who promised, over a decade ago, to help him to maintain the thatch. Much of the roof is now under plastic sheeting held down with assorted weights, huge chunks of metal and stones, contained here and there in incongruous plastic milk crates.

Many letters have gone back and forth, he explains – but to no avail. Fortunately Cairdean nan Taighean Tugha (Friends of the Thatched Houses) have decided to help with the restoration of the roof. This autumn, several hundred bundles of reeds have been cut from the field behind the house, and from up in the hills as well. The thatching material,

stacked to dry out, awaits the end of the stalking season when Duncan Matheson the stalker becomes the thatcher for a while.

The new thatch will make all the difference to the house and to how Donald feels about it. A calendar hanging in the parlour has not been turned since March 1985. It attests to the fact that he rarely sleeps over at No. 12 Ardelve now, preferring to share the company of his brother and niece in a larger house in Upper Ardelve.

When the fine weather returns next year and the roof has been restored, his visits, he says, might be more frequent. For him this is, of course, the house which stores treasured memories of the past in the collected clutter of china objects stuffed into the dresser, paintings and photographs, books and papers – everywhere he looks.

FLOURISHING FYVIE

A fortune amassed in the United States steel industry contributed to the Victorian flowering of one of Aberdeenshire's finest Renaissance strongholds. Fyvie Castle and its important collection of portraits and other works of art was purchased by the National Trust for Scotland in 1984, with the help of a generous grant from the National Heritage Memorial Fund. The Trust's curator, *David Learmont*, describes some of the dilemmas and delights encountered in the restoration of Fyvie's Victorian interiors now open for all to see.

The tower (above) is a memorial to one of the great families which shaped Fyvie Castle over six centuries, The Prestons, the Meldrums, the Setons, the Gordons and the Forbes-Leiths - with their architects, artists and craftsmen - all left their mark. The rehanging of the glittering eighteenth century chandelier (opposite) in the morning room symbolises Fyvie's most recent transformation.

The final flowering of Fyvie Castle came in the late 1880s when the property was purchased by Sir Alexander Forbes-Leith, later Lord Leith of Fyvie, a descendant of the Leith Hays of Leith Hall and the Prestons of Fyvie. Lord Leith, in addition to amassing a vast fortune in the United States steel industry, married an American heiress, Mary Louise January. The last tower was added in 1890 and Lord Leith refurbished the house in the opulent taste of the period.

Although the interior was redecorated between the wars, in recent years the house was hardly lived in. Very little furniture dating from the eighteenth century or earlier survived, since Lord Leith preferred to purchase new pieces in London which reflected seventeenth and eighteenth century styles, rather than to acquire genuine period furniture as a suitable complement to his outstanding collection of portraits. (These, together with his equally fine collection of arms and armour, were where his real interests lay.) The Trust therefore felt that the best over all approach was to present the castle's interiors as they might have appeared in the late nineteenth century.

The drawing room with the gallery beyond are the most striking of Fyvie Castle's interiors. In the eighteenth century this had been the morning room, but it was given more prominence when Lord Leith bought the castle and added the gallery. Like most of the castle the room had been redecorated between the wars and the Victorian red flock wallpaper had been removed in favour of a more contemporary wall covering. The chenille carpet, predominantly blue, green and red had faded considerably over the years, the red appearing as a fierce shade of orange. Since this would have jarred with the old red flock wallpaper, we decided to revert to the predominantly green eighteenth century colour

Lord Leith's library was recreated in the former dining room.

scheme. A fairly dark shade with an all over pattern was chosen as being suitable for a room which had been extensively remodelled in the 1890s and which also created an excellent background for eighteenth century pictures and furniture.

Lord Leith put up the elaborate plaster ceiling with its heraldic shields; this we repainted the original colour. Old red silk damask curtains, now recut for the back morning room, were replaced with new ones of the same colour, but this time cotton damask was used rather than silk to give longer life, and the tails of the pelmets were lined with green silk to match the wallpaper. The upholstery was left in its original state.

The pictures in the room are of outstanding quality; the portrait of William Gordon by Pompeo Batoni hangs between the windows, that of the Countess of Oxford by Lawrence over the chimney piece, and others by Gainsborough and Opie are notable examples. Important period furniture in the drawing room includes the eighteenth century open armchairs with needlework seats, a Continental commode and some early Georgian pier tables. These are supplemented by nineteenth century reproduction pieces of extremely high quality such as the

bureauplat in the centre of the room.

Leading out of the drawing room is the gallery at the top of the Leith Tower which Lord Leith added in 1890. The chimneypiece, dated 1521, is probably French and typical of the sort of purchase which rich collectors made at the end of the last century. The walls are hung with built-in tapestries woven from Rubens cartoons and the vaulted ceiling is enlivened with a simple geometric design. At the far end is an "organola" waiting to be restored. Apart from a repainted ceiling, the gallery has been left untouched.

Returning to the entrance hall – which was redecorated in the 1830s in the "modern antique style" which Sir Walter Scott made popular at Abbotsford and which at Fyvie Lord Leith retained and expanded – visitors today see a carefully restored ceiling enlivened at the intersections with repainted heraldic devices. The walls, painted a pinky grey in recent years, were changed to a traditional warm sand colour to tie in the ceiling with the large plaster relief depicting the Battle of Otterburn above the fireplace.

All the arms and armour were restored in the Trust's workshops in consultation with the Armouries at the Tower of London. Lord Leith had painstakingly catalogued his collection of arms and his arrangements had all been photographed, making it a straight-forward task to set up the displays as he had originally planned them.

Leading off the great wheel stair immediately above the billiard room is the dining room. This room, in the Gordon Tower, was built in the eighteenth century but had been completely altered in the 1890s. Plate glass windows replaced the original Georgian glazing bars earlier in the nineteenth century and Lord Leith installed dark oak panelling to dado level and doors with carved and moulded decoration. The chimneypiece was a tour de force made up from early barley sugar twist columns with, above, a built-in portrait of Mary Louise January in a boldly carved frame surmounted with his coat-of-arms. The ceiling was also completely replastered at this time in an elaborate Renaissance manner with pendants and heraldic devices.

The walls had been rehung between the wars with a drab straw paper. Fortunately a scrap of the nineteenth century red damask paper was found under some moulding and without going to vast expense we managed to find a similar paper printed on a large enough scale for such a lofty room. To have had a wallpaper specially printed would have

The gallery in the Leith Tower was added in 1890.

doubled the cost. This red damask paper is an ideal background for the collection of portraits in their gilt frames.

The dining room woodwork was freshened and the ceiling painted off-white with the heraldic shields touched up where necessary. The old tapestry curtains had faded and rotted down one side but they formed part of the 1890 rehabilitation scheme and we were determined to use them. The material was reversed, removing the rotted parts, and the curtains remade, fully lined and interlined to give extra body. A traditional chenille carpet had survived, and this was given a new lease of life with a contract quality underfelt.

All the furniture for this room

is nineteenth centry oak recalling various earlier styles: the dining table has Elizabethan legs, the serving tables have Tudor features and the chairs, inlaid with the coat-of-arms of Lord Leith, are an amalgam of seventeenth centry and Queen Anne. They were supplied by Frank Giles of London and had been covered in a fabric by Leigh of Birkenhead. Each was still in remarkably good condition thanks to their case covers which had also survived.

Climbing the wheel stair again, the visitor comes to the morning room. In the seventeenth century this was the high hall of the castle. During the eighteenth and most of the nineteenth it was the drawing room and, at some time in the last century, the fireplace was removed from the east to the south wall. Nearly all the furniture was retained by the family when the Trust purchased the castle, and we were left with a fine tapestry depicting a Fish Market, the pictures, a beautiful crystal chandelier and a truly hideous fitted carpet which the family themselves realised had been a ghastly mistake.

There was no question of trying to show this room as the Victorian drawing room that it had once been. For one thing, Lord Leith's drawing room survived at the top of the house, and for another, there was no spare furniture of that period to display in it. In reaching a compromise, we decided to furnish the room as a traditional, welcoming family sitting room. Easy chairs and friendly old furniture of no great merit were gathered from other parts of the house. The plaster ceiling was repainted a soft white and the panelling repaired and varnished just as it had been before.

The key was the purchase of a splendid oriental carpet which almost fitted the room exactly. Its colours became the basis for the chintz curtains and the sofa cover; the easy chairs were covered in plain material, two in pink and two in yellow; cushions made out of kelims were introduced to give a "lift". Throughout the house there was a considerable collection of blue and white Delft, and this was all assembled here where it was well set off by the panelling. The eighteenth centry chandelier was given more importance by lowering it twelve inches.

In recreating Lady Leith's boudoir, the Seton Room, the chair rail was reinstated and an old wallpaper pattern chosen along with a very traditional glazed chintz for the curtains and loose covers. An unusual old sofa, probably supplied by Lenygon and Morant, was brought in and the remaining pieces of furniture came from gifts and bequests in addition to a loan of furniture from the Royal Museum of Scotland. Some of the china on display was brought out of the china room and the rest came from a generous benefactor. The room is dominated by a portrait of Lord Leith's daughter and the remaining wall space is now closely hung with portraits, Victorian oil paintings and watercolours. An early telephone has been restored and placed on the writing desk where the blotter displays a seating arrangement for a dinner party at Fyvie.

When the Trust took the castle over, all the furniture had been removed from the library with the exception of a fine Regulator longcase clock. The modern carpet had to be replaced, but the curtains, although of comparatively recent date were acceptable. We decided to recreate Lord Leith's library in what had become a dining room although the decoration of his time had disappeared. Fortunately the nineteenth century bookcases with all the books had survived in the attics with the library pedestal desk and a suite of nineteenth century Chippendale style chairs.

There are two small turret rooms leading off the library, and here we found the Victorian wallpaper which once hung in the library. A close replica in both design and colour was obtained and the woodwork re-grained. The eighteenth century chimney-piece decorated with fruit and the steel grate dating from the 1890s had both survived intact but the grate required a thorough cleaning and restoration.

Once again old oriental carpets were laid on the floor. The chairs with their characteristic Victorian interior springing were re-covered in red haircloth. The walls are hung with two small tapestries, some early portraits and two handsome seascapes. The two turrets mentioned earlier have also been fully restored; one of them has become a small library fitted out with the remaining bookcases. The other, known as the Cabin, is devoted to Lord Leith's yachting interests.

The Dunfermline passage, linking the bedrooms on the second floor which reflect the Edwardian era of Fyvie, was in a sorry state, for although the grained ceiling had survived, all the remaining woodwork had been stripped. The walls were hung with seventeenth century tapestries, some exposed to sunshine, and these were in a very frail condition. Windows throughout the house have now been treated to reduce the ultra-violet light.

In order to give an otherwise undistinguished corridor more substance and restore its nineteenth century appearance, all the woodwork was oak grained by copying some existing graining on the staircase. The deep cream colour on the walls was retained and freshened. The tapestries, duly restored, were rehung, this time on the window wall away from the light, and seventeenth century portraits were double-hung on the opposite side. Unfortunately the old patterned linoleum had perished and it was not possible to replace it. A plain haircord and old runners were laid along the whole length of the corridor.

Now that the grand reception rooms have been restored, it is time for the Trust to move, as it were, behind the green baize door, and work backstairs. Renovation has started in the Victorian kitchen and pantry, and eventually a housekeeper's room and servants' bedrooms will be on public view as well. Meanwhile the treasures of Fyvie are being enjoyed and appreciated once more – and by many more people than in its heyday.

Interiors by Design Studio

Our stylish use of co-ordinated furnishings has become a hallmark of our design team. A telephone call to us is the first step in having the interior of your dreams successfully designed and executed.

Our showroom is full of lovely things and bright ideas. Come and see for yourself why we're called – Design Studio.

Our design team are always sensitive to the styles and period of any project. We can design and supply materials to suit the most traditional or avant-garde scheme . . . all beautifully put together by our caring staff.

From bedroom to bathroom our close attention to detail ensures a perfect balance of colour and texture. Choosing becomes a pleasure and one that is simplified by the help of our experienced staff.

We can design from drawings or simple sketches, we can pay you a visit, or you can visit us. Our aim is to see your scheme achieve its full potential of style and elegance that will give you pleasure for years to come.

All types of interiors can be undertaken, from bar to boardroom, from office to offshore accommodation. We can provide a full service from design to installation, which is carried out by tradesmen dedicated to providing the quality of finish for which we are now so well known.

·Design Studio·

**Bath Street and Bridge Street · Aberdeen ·
Telephone 0224 594684**

CHARLES HAMMOND FABRICS

Dysart, a Charles Hammond fabric at

DUNEDIN INTERIORS LTD

6 North West Circus Place, Edinburgh EH3 6ST, Scotland
Telephone 031-225 4874

SCOTTISH INTERIORS VICTORIAN STYLE

Janet Wilkie introduces sixty years of Victorian interior design – with a word of caution. The Victorian love of collected clutter and the profusion of styles which were the order of the day make it hard, after all, to say what is "typically Victorian".

Their mania for collecting, classifying and arranging a myriad of objects suggests one word in particular to sum up the interiors which the Victorians created - eclectic. These interiors - often dark, stuffy and over-crowded - both contained reminders of an enlarged range of interests, and demonstrated a need for security and comfort within a fast changing society.

To some extent this is explained by the avid study of history, the development of archaeology and the growth of tourism which went on throughout the century and led to a much wider and more informed appreciation of previous cultures than ever before.

Added to that, the impact of rapid developments in science and technology, the growth of industrial production and the Empire created a buoyant economy which enabled the newly wealthy middle classes to turn their social and domestic ambitions into reality.

During such a long reign as that of Queen Victoria, a number of styles of interior design and decoration evolved. In fact, the reign, from 1837-1901, conveniently divides into three eras corresponding to different phases of development of Victorian interior design and decoration: 1837-1851, 1851-1887 and 1887-1901. 1851 was the year of the Great Exhibition in London, that tremendous mid-century celebration of British achievement, and 1887 marks the year of Queen Victoria's Golden Jubilee.

The initial period from 1837 to 1851 was a time of rapid evolution from the purer classical styles of the Regency era, to the emergence of that extraordinary Victorian eclecticism. As early as 1829 the German architect and theorist Heinrich Hübsch had written an essay entitled *In what style should we build?* In 1848 the publication of Owen Jones's historical encyclopedia of decoration *The Grammar of Ornament* enabled designers to mix and match with authority, secure in the knowledge of their sources. Certain styles met with particular approval. The Gothic style of architecture and decoration had been selected by Sir Charles Barry for the rebuilding of the Houses of Parliament because it was thought to be British.

Scottish Victorian interiors had a style of their own, influenced by a number of factors including climate, light and differences in domestic architectural design and building materials. The immensely popular novels of Sir Walter Scott, together with Queen Victoria's selection of Balmoral Castle as her Highland home, promoted the Scottish Baronial style. This was interpreted decoratively in displays of armour and hunting trophies, such as sets of antlers, in a fashion for heavily carved psuedo-medieval furniture, and in the use of tartan, in furnishing fabrics and carpets. These elements influenced the furnishing and decoration of Scottish country houses and shooting lodges built by nouveau riche industrialists and members of the aristocracy. The armour was frequently displayed in baronial entrance halls, at Inveraray Castle and Blair Castle for example, while hunting trophies frequently graced the walls of male preserves like the billiard room.

At Glenquoich Lodge, Inverness-shire, built by the Rt. Hon. Edward Ellice, M.P. for Inverness-shire, the billiard room, with its pine matchboard dado, stained to imitate oak, had its upper walls punctuated by stags' heads, mounted and stuffed. Abbotsford, the internationally famous Border home of Sir Walter Scott, lent its name to the style of heavy carved oak furniture which frequently graced Scottish country house dining rooms and became especially popular with the development of carving machinery after 1851.

Such extravagances of scale and manner were impractical for the town dweller, but in conventional households the tendency to over-furnish persisted until the end of the century. Draperies were essential to the desired effect and from the 1840s onwards chimney pieces were swathed in material. Cassell's *Household Guide,* published in the early 1860s, explains how to create a mantel-board from a board laid over the mantel-shelf, covered with material, often velvet, and decorated with a matching flounce, which hung down over the front of the shelf. Also known as mantel-pelmets, these might be embroidered or beaded, and frequently matched other upholstery in the room. In summer arrangements, the look might be carried further, with the chimney piece being hung with curtains, in lace or muslin, drawn back to reveal a flower arrangement or cluster of potted plants arranged on the hearth, inside the fender.

During the 1870s and 1880s more advanced circles responded to the stylistic influences of the Arts and Crafts and Aesthetic Movements. Theorists like Charles Eastlake reacted against the elaborate ornamentation of previous decades. His book, *Hints on Household Taste,* published in 1868, and Robert Edis's *The Decoration and Furniture of Town Houses,* published in 1881, explained how to achieve the new look.

Eastlake, and his contemporary Bruce Talbert, championed the return to the Gothic Revival, with its emphasis on honesty of form and construction, and sound workmanship. Talbert's *Gothic Forms applied to Furniture, Metalwork and Decoration for Domestic Purposes* appeared in London in 1867. Like Eastlake, he favoured the use of colour. Furniture inspired by him was designed in the Gothic manner, with colour used in bold and striking combinations. Both Eastlake and Talbert echoed the approach of William Morris and his associates Philip Webb, an architect, and the painters Dante Gabriel Rossetti and Sir Edward Burne-Jones, who had together founded the firm of Morris, Marshall, Faulkner & Co., in 1861.

The evolution of Morris's firm epitomises the transition in taste from 1860 to the turn of the century. In the first phase of the company's development - to 1875 - there was an emphasis on heavy, sturdily made, simple pieces of furniture, some of which, like those designed by Ford Madox Brown, were stained dark green. Others, similar to those designed by William Burges for Lord Bute at Cardiff Castle, were elaborately decorated. From the 1880s onwards there was a greater production of upholstered furniture, and during the 1890s, they even turned to reproducing antique Chippendale designs of the eighteenth century.

Right through Victoria's reign technological improvements and inventions swelled the large range of household goods available. Rather like today, it was possible to create an enormous range of impressions in interior decoration. The cross section of Victorian interiors included in this volume - from the croft house to Mount Stuart - demonstrates this well and gives pause for thought when the phrase "typically Victorian" comes to mind.

VICTORIA'S FAVOURITE FABRICS

Chintz, velvets and silks, Paisley patterns and tartans are available today in stylish new guises.

Tartan and thistle-patterned chintz in Queen Victoria's sitting room at Balmoral Castle, 1857. Lithograph by Vincent Brooks.

Grand Victorian rooms invited lavish use of fabrics - chintz, velvets and silks were favourites - and inventions in the textile industry made their mass manufacture possible. Patterned chintz and tartan were introduced to Balmoral in 1855 as Lady Augusta Bruce notes in her diary: ". . . the carpets are Royal Stewart tartan and green Hunting Stewart, the curtains, the former lined with red, the same Dress Stewart and a few chintz with a thistle pattern, the chairs and sofas in the drawing room are Dress Stewart poplin. All highly characteristic and appropriate, but not all equally *flatteux* to the eye".

"Chintz" derives from an Indian word and is now used interchangeably with "glazed cotton". The fabric was originally manufactured in India for export to Europe where it has been popular

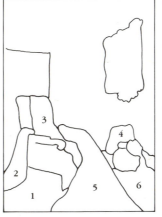

Opposite: the Victorian Room created by the Fine Art Society in Edinburgh - a perfect setting for showing-off modern equivalents of old favourites.

1 'Griffin': cotton resembling chenille velvet. Osborne & Little.
2 and 3 'Penjab' and 'Kalif': traditional Paisley designs in fine cotton. Whytock & Reid.
4 'Grand Paisley': cotton. Laura Ashley.
5 'Scherzo': cotton. Liberty & Co.
6 'Albert': cotton, Laura Ashley.

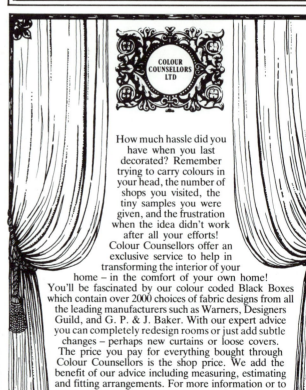

Butterflies and glorious garden blooms captured on a black background. 'Tasmin': continental chintz, from Whytock & Reid.

since the seventeenth century and associated with the relaxed elegance of the country house. Paisley pattern, another Victorian favourite, developed from Kashmir floral motifs which by the end of the eighteenth century took the form of a stylised cone and, later, a formal scroll-like motif in an all-over pattern.

In the form of fine-woven "Cashmere" shawls, the textiles became popular and are highly valued today. Edinburgh was a major centre of manufacture and the first to imitate Kashmir patterns in a brocade-weaving technique. The shawl industry in Paisley, which became the British centre of manufacture,

started as an offshoot of the Edinburgh industry and was the first to use the Jacquard loom in 1833.

Here is a selection of up-to-the-minute fabrics - some from the new collections of top manufacturers - all inspired by the Victorian era. It includes the 'Ardgowan House Collection' reproduced by Ramm, Son & Crocker. Trunks in the attic of Ardgowan House on Clydeside were recently found to be full of Victorian furnishings. The fabrics were carefully wrapped and marked with details of the rooms where they once hung. An inventory of 1843 evokes Ardgowan as "typically" Victorian - cosy and cluttered!

SCOTTISH STOCKISTS

C P & J BAKER: Inside Story, Interiors by PWD, Town & Country Designs, David Cole, John MacGregor, Dorothy Quin Interiors, James L Archibald, Decor (Aberdeen), Alistair Reid, Anderson & England, Alex Anderson, Martins, Curtain Boutique, A F Drysdale, Galloways, Martin & Frost, Remus, Swags & Tails, Whytock & Reid, Jan's Fabric Boutique, Hunters Furnishing, Gabbi Fabrics, David Gibson, Art Fabrics, T Connell, Designworks, M Bruce Jeffrey, Town House Country House, Joni Ancill, Gryffe Interiors, George Tannahill, James T Young, Northwood Designs, Alan Beaton, Two's Company, Thomas Love.

CHARLES HAMMOND: Sylvia Lawson Johnston, Joy Jack, Thomas Love, Alister Reid, Remus, Treliganus, Two's Company, Whytock & Reid, Alison Wilson, Northwood Designs, Andjan, Sarah Law, Adam McNee, Dunkeld Interiors, Hamilton and Burt, Laura Harrison, Sunderland Hall, C & C Designs, Joni Ancill, Art Fabrics, A F Drysdale, Dunedin Interiors, Farr Furnishing, Gabbi Fabrics, Wendy Gray, Katie Guest, Estelle Haddy, Interiors by PWD.

RAMM SON & CROCKER: Joni Ancill, Estelle Haddy, Northwood Designs, Adam McNee, C & C Designs, Sunderland Hall, A F Drysdale, Remus, Whytock & Reid, Victoria Street Designs, Alistair Reid.

Joni Ancill Interiors, 6 Mains Ave, Eastwood Toll, Giffnock.
Alex Anderson, 63 Market Pl, Inverurie.
Anderson & England Ltd, 50 Lossie Wynd, Elgin.
Andjan Ltd, 438 Hillington Rd, Glasgow.
James L Archibald & Sons, 6/14 Great Western Rd, Aberdeen.
Alan Beaton Interior Design, 140 Perth Rd, Dundee.
C & C Designs, 5 Queen's Court, Sandgate, Ayr.
David Cole, 71 Queensferry St, Dumfries.
T Connell, 2 Allison St, Glasgow.
The Curtain Boutique, 46 Marionville Rd, Edinburgh.
Decor of Aberdeen, 157 Skene St, Aberdeen.
Designworks, 34 Gibson St, Glasgow.
Dunkeld Interiors, 14 Bridge St, Dunkeld.
Farr Furnishings, Craggan, Granton-on-Spey.
Gabbi Fabrics, Knockbuckle House, 2 Barrmill Rd, Beith.
David Gibson (Carpets), Burghill Pl, Bridge of Weir.
Wendy Gray, Spylaw Bank, Spylaw Ave, Edinburgh.
Gryffe Interiors, Market Pl, Kilmacolm.
Katie Guest Designs, 13 Ainslie Pl, Edinburgh.
Estelle Haddy Interiors, 86 High St, Auchterarder.
Hamilton and Burt, Auldhame, North Berwick.
Laura Harrison, Bystone Peel Rd, Thornton Hall, Glasgow.
Hunters Furnishing International, Newton Trading Est, Ayr.
Inside Story, Main St, Chirnside, Berwickshire.
Joy Jack Interiors, 86 King St, Castle Douglas.
Jans Fabric Boutique, 56 Raeburn Pl, Edinburgh.
M Bruce Jeffrey (Carpets) Ltd, 574 Clarkston Rd, Glasgow.
Sarah Law Interior Design, 16 Rothesay Mews, Edinburgh.
Sylvia Lawson Johnston, 137 Union Grove, Aberdeen.
John MacGregor of St Andrews Ltd, 73 Market St, St Andrews.
Adam McNee Interior Design, 50 George St, Perth.
Martin & Frost, 83/85 George St, Edinburgh.
Martins Ltd, 10 Academy St, Inverness.
Northwood Designs, Trinity Gask, Auchterarder.

Dorothy Quin Interiors, 121 South St, St Andrews.
Alistair Reid Furnishings Ltd, 21 Rubislaw Terr, Aberdeen.
Remus, 18 Stafford St, Edinburgh.
Sunderland Hall Designs, Galashiels, Selkirkshire.
Swags & Tails, 7 Jeffrey St, Edinburgh.
George Tannahill & Sons, 75-79 John Finnie St, Kilmarnock.
Town & Country Designs, 16 Balfron Rd, Killearn.
Town House, Country House, 458-462 Crow Rd, Glasgow.
Treliganus, Broich, Doune, Perthshire.
Interiors by PWD, 50 Woolmarket, Kelso.
Alison Wilson, Peilton, Moniaive, Thornhill, Dumfriesshire.
James T Young & Co, 20 Templehill, Troon.

Details of stockists not listed above appear in Janet Wilkie's Address List, pp. 84-85.

Left: *Charles Hammond's 'Landseer' chinz photographed with a mock-Landseer painting (regrettably, not for sale) at the Fine Art Society, Edinburgh.*

Below: *The Ardgowan House Collection in glazed cotton: Springkell, Moreen, Lucinda and Lady Octavia. Ramm Son & Crocker Ltd.*

Opposite:
1 *'Paisley': cotton Laura Ashley.*
2 *'Genoa': crushed cotton velvet. Osborne & Little.*
3 *'Nantes': Upholstery weight cotton. C.P. & J. Baker.*
4 *'Carmen': Tamesa Silk Collection. Osborne & Little.*
5 *'Kabul': cotton. Parkertex at Remus.*
6 *'Taffeta': Tamesa Silk Collection. Osborne & Little.*

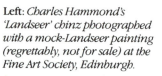

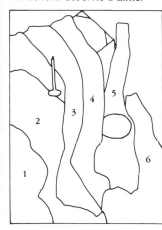

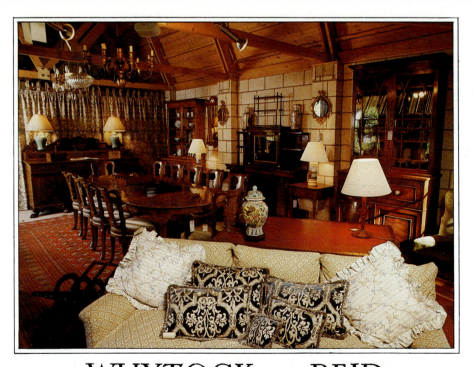

78

PUTTING ON THE STYLE

Victoria Street Designs decorated this East Lothian cottage bedroom with a profusion of antique lace and Wemyss Ware.

An exciting variety of up-to-the-minute furnishings and fittings can be collected and arranged by modern enthusiasts of the Victorian style. *Janet Wilkie* passes on ideas and sources of inspiration in her invaluable guide.

Anyone contemplating the re-creation of a Victorian interior today, should begin with some research. Examine the building in question and the title deeds if they are available; find out when it was built and whether it is individual or part of a group. Try to look at similar properties in the area, to identify comparable original features.

Having established the period of your house, look at its present plan, and at the details and proportions of its fixtures and fittings. The plan may well have changed, with the addition of bathrooms and the removal of the kitchen to a different location, for example. Most owners nowadays will opt for certain compromises, particularly in fitting kitchens and bathrooms.

Do not be seduced into thinking that it is necessary to have a fitted kitchen. A scrubbed pine table, freestanding dresser, and a range of appropriately designed cupboards may well provide a good solution, especially for the more spacious kitchen. Consider, too, the late Victorian - and still

A bedroom decorated in 'Camellia Ribbon' fabrics and wallpapers from Osborne & Little's 'Arcadia' collection.

popular - central island which combines surfaces for food preparation with storage and cooking facilities. Depending on location, choose a solid fuel stove for both heating and cooking or separate hobs and ovens.

A number of companies are now manufacturing reproduction Victorian suites and fittings, such as B.C. Sanitan, Original Bathrooms and the British Bathroom Centre. Brass taps and fittings, and reproduction Victorian tiles are all part of the look. The art tile company, Muton of Paris, reproduces a number of attractive designs, and others are available from Minton and through such London stockists as Paris Ceramics and World's End Tiles. Flooring is important in both kitchens and bathrooms. Here, for easy maintenance, I would suggest good quality vinyl tiles, as produced by Amtico, or Fired Earth's earthenware tiles. Resist the temptation to over-decorate either room. Festoon blinds were distinctly old-fashioned by the early nineteenth century, and simple roller blinds are more in keeping. Lace curtains -

several manufacturers reproduce attractive Nottingham lace designs - would soften bathroom windows.

Depending on the date of your house, decorative paint effects and stencilling may be appropriate. The wallpaper manufacturer Cowtan noted that in 1883 graining was in demand - maple for drawing rooms, oak or walnut for libraries. Stencilling, encouraged by the Gothic Revival of the 1860s, continued to be a popular alternative to a printed border at cornice and dado level.

After 1880, it became popular to divide the wall into three components: frieze, filling and dado. Embossed papers such as 'Lincrusta', invented in 1877 and 'Anaglypta' became popular for dados. Crown Wallcoverings are amongst a number of companies manufacturing similar papers today, although if authenticity is the aim, take care about the choice of design. For a refreshing contemporary interpretation the 'Sirius' and 'Arcadia' range of wallpapers and co-ordinating fabrics from Osborne & Little are worth considering,

'Candle Chestnut', another example from the 'Arcadia' collection.

although these papers are flat rather than embossed. Laura Ashley have also reproduced several original designs by Owen Jones, including a small diamond diaper design, which can work well as a dado paper.

While contemporary versions of Victorian papers may well be acceptable for extensive staircase walls and bedrooms, enthusiasts for authenticity may want to invest in accuracy for their main reception rooms. Four London-based manufacturers - Cole & Son, Hamilton Weston, Tissunique and Watts & Co. - all reproduce nineteenth century wallpapers, and can offer a custom-made service to reproduce historic fragments of original wallpaper, although this is naturally extremely expensive. Many of their designs are still hand-printed. Contemporary alternatives include the reprints of William Morris designs available from Sanderson, and Liberty's range of wallpapers and borders which co-ordinate with their attractive and authentically late-Victorian furnishing fabric designs.

For the sake of comfort and practicality, when heating, lighting and flooring are under consideration, compromises are likely to occur. It is now possible to buy reproductions of Victorian coil radiators, while a number of companies specialise in salvaging and restoring Victorian fireplaces. It is well worth investigating architectural salvage companies for both fireplaces, radiators and light fittings. The Edinbugh New Town Conservation Committee runs a salvage yard, while Mr Purves's Lighting Emporium in Stockbridge, Edinburgh is a treasure trove of antique light fittings and spare components.

Appropriate lighting is crucial to the mood and effectiveness of a Victorian interior. Consider the possibility of installing small spotlight downlighters set into the ceiling, to complement the effect of a central adjustable pendant fitting or lamps, for example. For atmosphere and effect, the Victorian houseowner may well decide on a combination of oil lamps and candle light. Throughout the nineteenth century, candles continued to be used on the dinner table, especially when entertaining, and on mantelpieces.

Remember that the Victorians were great collectors of objects from the past, as well as emulating its styles. Georgian silver or Sheffield plate candlesticks and candelabra continued to be used throughout the century. On mantelpieces, garnitures (combinations of candlesticks and ornaments) were popular from the early nineteenth century onwards, the suite sometimes consisting of a clock in the centre, with matching obelisks or vases, and candlesticks as an addition or an alternative.

Symmetrical grouping and arrangement of ensembles was all-important. For the mid and late nineteenth century grand dinner table, silver plate candelabra might be combined with an elaborate centrepiece. Take care over the choice of candles: coloured ones are a twentieth century affectation. Good quality beeswax candles, an attractive deep cream in colour, are preferable.

Flooring is important to the authentic appearance of a Victorian interior. Fitted carpets only began to be used at the end of the century. Prior to that, wooden board or parquet floors were more frequent, covered with rugs or bordered carpets, often of Wilton or Axminster weaves. The original Wilton and Axminster factories still survive, at Wilton, near Salisbury, and at Axminster, in Devon. Several carpet companies, such as Woodward Grosvenor, Craigie Stockwell and Hugh Mackay of Durham offer special facilities in reweaving historic designs. However, auction sales may, with care, provide a less expensive solution. Persian and Turkish carpets are certainly suitable. There was an extensive specialist carpet weaving industry in Persia, catering for European demand, and Turkey red carpets were popular in many mid-Victorian drawing rooms. Hand-tufted occasional rugs and rag rugs also became popular. Rag rugs, made during long winter evenings, can still be imitated, to provide the cheapest form of carpeting of all, attractive for fireside or bedside use, especially in a cottage setting.

Drapery is a key ingredient of Victorian interior decoration. Elaborate styles of curtains and pelmets remained popular until late in the century. Felix Lenoir's *Practical and Theoretical Treatise on Decorative Hangings or the Guide to Upholstery* was published in Brussels and London in 1890. It proposed lavish uses of fabric, with draped pelmets continuing between windows, and even swag and tail drapes above portraits. The curtains themselves might be asymmetrically arranged, caught by corded and tasselled tie-backs. An alternative to this extravagance was to use simpler, heavier curtains in chenille or velvet, often with embroidered edging panels, suspended from rings on curtain poles. This form of arrangement was popular for doors, providing portieres, as door curtains were called, to protect against draughts. Venetian and roller blinds were used, the latter sometimes painted with decorative border designs, but note again, festoon and Roman blinds were out of fashion.

Auction sales are a good hunting ground for curtains, bedlinen and furniture. Again, do research beforehand. Consult auction firms' staff about the best sales to attend and likely price ranges. Go to a number of sales, and their preliminary viewing days, as an observer, to get a feel of the trade - and beware being pushed up to inflated prices. Lyle's *Price Guide to Antiques* gives an accurate idea of current prices.

Despite the fun and excitement of auction sales, they can

force *Authentic Decor 1660-1920*, Susan Lasdun's *Victorians At Home* and Caroline Davidson's *The World of Mary Ellen Best* are all entertaining and highly informative, with numerous contemporary illustrations of Victorian interiors. Magazines such as *Traditional Interior Decoration* provide a fund of information.

Finally, remember that Victorian interiors were frequently crowded with carefully arranged groups of pictures, drawings, prints and photographs. The example par excellence of this is Linley Sambourne House in London, the Victorian home of the Punch cartoonist, now run by the Victorian Society as a house museum. Visits to National Trust for Scotland and Historic Houses Association houses of the period, which are open to the public, are sure to inspire and enlighten the enthusiast.

Depending on the type of your house, and budget, you

also be distracting, and may lead to unintentional purchases. For specific requirements, it is well worth while cultivating reliable local antique dealers, who may then search for appropriate items. A number of Scottish dealers in Victorian furniture is cited at the end of this article, although the list is by no means exhaustive.

In the re-creation of Victorian interiors detail and grouping of arrangements are particularly important. Study the photographs of Cardy House, to see how ensembles have been built up. Books like Peter Thornton's invaluable tour de

Top left: conservatories enabled the Victorians to indulge their love of plants and are enjoying a revival today. Marston & Langinger of Norfolk produce authentic, high-quality designs. The one above contains a cast iron table and wicker furniture in addition to all that verdant foliage.

left: hexagonal terracotta tiles like these, imported from France by Paris Ceramics, make hard-wearing and attractive flooring for Victorian style kitchens.

'Katimar': A selection of Paisley designs in cotton by Sekers Ltd.

may opt for a spacious display of paintings and objets d'art. Galleries such as The Fine Art Society in Edinburgh and Glasgow, Edinburgh's Calton Gallery and Bourne Fine Art, The Washington Gallery in Glasgow and the McEwan Gallery in Ballater, are all worth trying for nineteenth century paintings and prints. The Fine Art Society also specialises in high quality Scottish furniture and Victorian decorative art objects, including ceramics and glass, and metalwork by the remarkable Victorian botanist turned designer Christopher Dresser.

The Architectural Heritage Society of Scotland, and the Scottish Group of the Furniture History Society are organisations which organise visits to interesting houses in private ownership, including a number of Victorian properties.

Buying a Victorian house and restoring it may well become a life-time interest and commitment and the effort entailed will be amply rewarded.

JANET WILKIE'S ADDRESS LIST

FABRICS & WALLPAPERS
Art Fabrics
146 West Regent Street
Glasgow
041-248 3322

Victoria Street Designs
16 Victoria Street
Edinburgh
031-225 5714

Liberty
47 George Street
Edinburgh EH2
031-226 5491

Laura Ashley
137 George Street
Edinburgh
031-225 1121
and
215 Sauchiehall Street
Glasgow
041-333 0850

A F Drysdale
35 North West Circus Place
Edinburgh EH3
031-225 4686

Galloways
St Stephen Street
Edinburgh EH3
031-225 3221

Osborne & Little
39 Queen Street
Edinburgh EH2
031-225 5068

Two's Company
17 Murray Street
Montrose
0674 72851

Design Studio
Bath Street and Bridge Street
Aberdeen 0224 594684

Colour Counsellors
Measuring, estimating, fitting, sample selection and interior design, in the convenience of your own home Look in Yellow Pages for local Counsellor or ring Colour Counsellors, London, 01 736-8326/7 for information.

ORIENTAL RUGS
Martin & Frost
83-85 George Street
Edinburgh EH2
031-225 2933

PAINT
Craig & Rose
172 Leith Walk
Edinburgh
031-554 1131

FIREPLACES
Dunedin Antiques
6 North West Circus Place
Edinburgh EH3
031-225 3074

Cinders
51 St Stephen Street
Edinburgh EH3
031-225 3743

TILES
Douglas Hunter
4 Harestanes Cottages
Ancrum
Roxburghshire
08353 328

Bill Purves in his Stockbridge lighting emporium.

John Burgess Tiles
Maws Craft Centre
Jackfield
Shropshire
0952 884094

**BRUSHES AND
WOODEN UTENSILS**
Robert Cresser
40 Victoria Street
Edinburgh
031-225 2181

ART GALLERIES
The Fine Art Society
134 Blythswood Street
Glasgow
041-332 4027
and
12 Great King Street
Edinburgh EH3
031-556 0305

Calton Gallery
10 Royal Terrace
Edinburgh
031-556 1010

Bourne Fine Art
4 Dundas Street
Edinburgh EH3
031-557 4050

The Washington Gallery
44 Washington Street
Glasgow
041-221 6780

The McEwan Gallery
Ballater
0338 55429

The Rendezvous Gallery
100 Forest Avenue
Aberdeen
0224 323247

AUCTION HOUSES
Lyon & Turnbull
51 George Street
Edinburgh EH2
031-225 4627

Christies
164-166 Bath Street
Glasgow
041-332 8134

Phillips Fine Art Auctioneers
65 George Street
Edinburgh EH2
031-225 2266

Sotheby's
112 George Street
Edinburgh EH2
031-226 7201

**REPRODUCTION
FURNITURE**
Shapes Furniture
33 West Mill Road
Edinburgh EH13
031-441 79

Pine Country
14 Springvalley Gardens
Edinburgh EH10
031-447 5795
and
52 Holburn Street
Aberdeen
0224 572540

ANTIQUES
David Letham
17a Dundas Street
Edinburgh EH3
031-557 4466

Aldric Young
49 Thistle Street
Edinburgh EH2
031-226 4101

Lovatt Antiques
100 Torrisdale Steet
Glasgow
01-423 6497

The Victorian Village
53,57 & 63 West Regent Street
Glasgow
041-332 6703
041-332 0808

Crown Arcade Antiques
33 Virginia Street
Glasgow
041-552 8957

Atholl Antiques
322 Great Western Road
Aberdeen
0224 593547

Colin Wood Antiques
25 Rose Street
Aberdeen
0224 643019

Perth Antique Centre
28 Glasgow Road
Perth
0738 37473

Carse Antiques
Rait by Perth
08217 205

Elizabeth Paterson Antiques
1a Main Street
Bannockburn
0786 816392

Alistair Reid (Furnishings) Ltd.

21 Rubislaw Terrace,
Aberdeen AB1 1XE
Telephone: 0224-641955

**INTERIOR DECORATION &
GENERAL FURNISHINGS**
Whytock & Reid
Sunbury House
Belford Mews
Edinburgh
031-226 4911

Thomas Love & Sons
6 South Street
John's Place
Perth
0738 24111

LIGHTING
Mr Purves's Lighting Emporium
59 St Stephen Street
Edinburgh EH3
031-556 7054

R.& S.Robertson
44 Queen Street
Edinburgh
031- 226 4750

**RELEVANT
ORGANISATIONS**
The Furniture History Society
c/o The Dept of Furniture and
Interior Design
Victoria & Albert Museum
Cromwell Road
London SW7

The Architectural Heritage
Society of Scotland
43b Manor Place
Edinburgh
031-225 9724

The National Trust for Scotland
5 Charlotte Square
Edinburgh
031-226 5922

Historic Houses Association
38 Ebury Street
London SW1
Tel: 01-730 9410

**Conservation Bureau
Scottish Development Agency**
Rosebery House
Edinburgh
031-337 9595

The Victorian Society
1 Priory Gardens
Bedford Park
London W4
01-994 1019

ARCHITECTURAL SALVAGE
**Edinburgh New Town
Conservation Committee**
13a Dundas Street
Edinburgh EH3
031-556 7054

Exclusive hand polished solid mahogany or fine veneered tables for the boardroom or the home.

shapes

Colour brochure now available illustrating a sample of our new office and domestic range.

**Largest display of quality reproduction furniture in Scotland.
Over 3000 pieces on display or in stock.
Leasing facilities now available for all office furniture.**

Showroom, 6 West Mill Road, (off Woodhall Road)
Colinton, Edinburgh 031 441 7963
Open 7 days 9—5 p.m. Sunday 12—5 p.m.

All retail and office or hotel contract enquiries welcome.
Export orders taken for worldwide distribution.
Custom built furniture for the discerning.

SOUTHGATE

The Picturesque Interior of an 'Amateur House Decorator'.
Ian Gow relates the story of the Edinburgh Rector who rebelled against
mahogany and horsehair and furnished his villa with antiques.

In 1882 John Marshall, M.A., Barrister at Law of Lincoln's Inn, came to Edinburgh to take up the prestigious Rectorship of the Royal High School. In keeping with his new status, he acquired a suitably large house - "Southgate" in Craigmillar Park, a fashionable villa-quarter. Unusually, he proceeded to supervise its furnishing himself, instead of entrusting the task to the appropriate tradesmen. Far from being branded an eccentric, Southgate was so much admired that he was asked to lecture to the Edinburgh Architectural Society in April 1883. His paper, as befitted a classicist and a barrister, was both stylish and persuasively argued, and the society moved that it should be printed. Entitled *Amateur House Decoration*, it was published in October with "illustrations, from sketches taken in the Author's house".

A century later, Marshall's amusing essay provides an important document for the student of Victorian taste. The illustrations offer a fascinating survey of an Edinburgh suburban villa - albeit an untypical one. Anxious to shake off the smug philistinism of the early Victorian home, Marshall's solution was to furnish Southgate with antiques. To explain how his "love of antiques" had arisen, Marshall set out "to string together a sort of autobiographical thread of personal domestic experience." The result is a vivid satire on the banalities of conventional taste.

The "domestic auto-biography" opens in "a little house in London where my first household altar was set up some ten or eleven years ago" - furnished by "the ogre calling himself the upholsterer":

"It was of the usual conventional type, with, in the dining-room, the regulation set of mahogany chairs with morocco seatings; the sideboard all bossed with fruits and flowers, mechanically carved and casually glued, and the big mirror behind, so arranged that the light from the window lost all its shadow, and the room was converted, by uncomfortable reflections, into an uneasy chamber of doppel-gangers; green rep curtains on the windows, dark red Brussels carpet all over the floor - all very handsome and costly and, to one's present sight, abominable. The drawing-room with its round centre table, neatly bearing in a kind of wheel-spoke pattern, layers of albums and other polite literature; its bright red carpet, over which large flowers of white and yellow impossibly disported; its Nottingham lace curtains, two yards sprawling on the floors; and above all, the "splendid" chiffonier, with its "noble" glass above a noble slab of marble, and its three doors beneath, each with its sheet of plate glass reflecting your boots and lower integuments in pleasing detachment from the reflection of your waistcoat above. Who has not seen all this - who may not see its like in thousands of decent households here and elsewhere?"

Marshall's independent spirit began to assert itself on this background as he tired of this etiquette-book in horsehair and mahogany, with its stultified furniture arrangement: "The first vague instincts of personal feeling in regard to one's rooms took the form of a rather restless and seemingly aimless shifting about of the pieces. The round table got successively into every corner of the drawing-room, was finally turned up on its edge, and then shifted out altogether, as useless in a room intended for sitting in. The sideboard was moved into the morning-room, and replaced by a dwarf bookcase of quite terrific character; carved supports of aggravated kind, with lions' heads and bulbous fruits, and all agreeably lacquered over with varnish to the required antique depth. Antimacassars began to disappear as nuisances; the Nottingham lace curtains were replaced by cretonne and so forth."

"The next stage" towards his assumption of personal control over his environment was china mania. "One began to haunt all kinds of dingy shops; take deep interest in Worcester, and Bow and Chelsea and Lowestoft, and the wall above the bookcase aforesaid, and up each side of the mantel-glass and elsewhere, began to blossom out in arrays of plates, from which plaster and paper suffered terribly; and eccentricity at least was in some sort, attained." Looking back, Marshall realised that his appreciation of the pretty decorative enamel tints of the china had been an educational experience: "blindly enough, one was feeling after colour", which enabled him to savour to the full the final formative experience:

"Then came the great event - one's introduction to a really beautiful drawing-room, very tiny, but done by an artist. A little Louis Seize clock in white and gold, on its bracket; a graceful wooden mantel with its festoons and vases in delicate grey; a Persian carpet on the floor; a pretty oval table with Sheraton legs and shell inlaid, on which was an oriental vase converted into a lamp; some few Chippendale chairs and couch in delicate bronze velvet; and a little Broadwood grand piano. Walls of French grey and gold picked out in a creamy white, with some artistic sketches in water and oil here and there, the whole centred by an escritoire of Sheraton make, in satinwood. The tout ensemble produced such a confusion, such a delightful pell mell of new ideas, and left me nearly dumb with joy as of a new birth."

If we compare this room with the earlier description of the London one there are two major differences. The latter is

not only equipped with "antiques" but has a much more subtle colour scheme. On returning home Marshall himself "felt the whole thing was a hopeless horror." However, fate now intervened:

"Luckily for me I was called on to remove to Oxford, which gave me the excuse for a general elimination of all our wretched household gods, except some heretofore despised old tables and chairs that had lingered neglected in bedrooms, now to reappear with the honour they deserved in our re-constructed Oxford drawing-room."

In other words, in emulation of the room he so much admired, Marshall was becoming a confirmed antique collector. Compared with the work of the revered Chippendale and Sheraton, the debased rococo furniture of his own day was merely "the ultimate bathos of fashions that grew out of and at last destroyed one of the most splendid styles of furniture decoration the world has ever seen." Though framed as an aesthetic preference, and even an economy since there were then few collectors to compete against, Marshall was unaware of the extent to which his love for antiques was almost absurdly romantic. He fondly dwells on the charms of old family houses where every object was redolent of events in family history. During his Oxford period he began to surround himself with a picturesque array of antiques.

His personal experience however, proved that modern life mediated against the long occupation of a single house and one more move brought him and a van-load of antiques to the brash vulgarity of Southgate, a typical speculative builder's bay-fronted villa whose awkward planning was complete with all the pretentious appointments that he now despised. He would certainly have concurred with Robert Louis Stevenson's dismissal of Edinburgh's Victorian villas "as belonging to no style of art, only to a form of business much to be regretted". If he was unable to alter the architecture, he could at least arrange the interior to suit his personal taste. As Marshall admitted, however, it took "courage" to reject the social conventions of the standard Victorian interior, and it is interesting that he was also to take an active part in various social reforms during his time in Edinburgh.

The book illustrates three rooms. The entrance hall has "Queen Anne" detailing which may have been introduced by Marshall himself to provide a more suitable background to the collection. Instead of the regulation suite of hall chairs and combination lobby table and hat stand, which an upholsterer would deem essential, Marshall has substituted a pair of infinitely more picturesque Charles II high-backed chairs and "an old inlaid linen chest which may well decorate our hall and accommodate our boots or gloves."

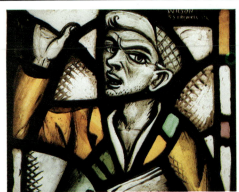
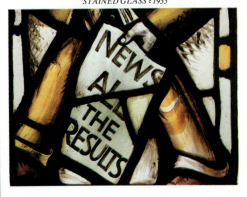
A vignette of the dining room shows that he installed mouldings round the upper walls of his rooms to recall the low ceilings of his Oxford rooms, which he missed. The frieze thus produced, prefigures a standard component in late nineteenth century decoration. The Jacobean buffet must be an Oxford purchase, but the Sheraton sideboard has a high superstructure of standard Scottish type and may have been bought in Edinburgh. The dining chairs, almost inevitably, are Chippendale in style. Marshall warned his readers against slavishly adopting a single historical theme since the results could only be as unpicturesque as a room fitted out all at once with an upholsterer's "twenty guinea suite."

We then move upstairs to what the builder had intended as the drawing room. Since in Marshall's system a pretentious drawing room had no place, it was arranged rather as the "Music Room" with the piano emphatically placed in the centre to underline this message. Surrounding it are representative examples covering the entire history of Georgian furniture, and Marshall has substituted a fine carved antique chimneypiece for the builder's cold white marble slabs. With rigourous thoroughness the very textiles are antique. Eschewing the standard fitted carpets, Marshall arranged antique rugs on a dark varnished floor, chosen to show them off. His table covers, and even the curtains, are made from carefully selected old fabrics.

Surprisingly, in view of his "amateur" status, Marshall awards full credit for the final effect to the services of a "professional decorator". It is tempting to identify this un-named collaborator as Thomas Bonnar who played a leading part in the Edinburgh Architectural Association and may have invited Marshall to lecture after their happy collaboration on Southgate. Recently two photographs in the National Monuments Record of Scotland were identified as views of Southgate which give a much sharper picture of the house than the line drawings which illustrated the lecture. The drawing room's frieze (page 88) is not a wallpaper, but a stencilled band of the Japanese chrysanthemums beloved by the Aesthetic Movement, which with the restrained wallpaper form an appropriate background to the pictures. Mrs Marshall advertised her services as a portrait painter and the photograph shows that they possessed a collection of modern pictures which gave the final artistic polish to Southgate.

The second photograph (page 89) illustrates part of the drawing room's bay window and is notably atmospheric, capturing something of the excitement which the house provided in 1883. A Hepplewhite work table has been pressed into service as a picturesque plant stand, whose leafage is set off against an almost Firbankian ancient velvet vestment. A long case clock substitutes for the standard marble timepiece in the centre of the chimney shelf in the average drawing room. A piece of antique damask has been arranged as a draw-up festoon curtain, letting as much light in as possible; and there are souvenirs of his china mania, Persian rugs and no less than three Chippendale chairs.

Marshall defended his love of antiques from the accusation that it was "merely a craze." A hundred years later he would be delighted to learn that it was still a potent force in contemporary decoration and amused to know that his despised early-Victorian furnishings have now acquired a picturesque charm as well.

RLS'S BATHROOM

Modern household plumbing represents a triumph of technology
which took more than a century to evolve. Even for prosperous late
Victorians, the bathroom was often far from being a place of sweetness and light,
as Robert Louis Stevenson's Californian wife, Fanny, discovered. *Fay Young* reports
on progress in the 'smallest room' of the Stevenson house.

The lack of plumbing at 17 Heriot Row amazed Fanny, Robert Louis Stevenson's Californian wife, when she came to his Edinburgh home for the first time in 1880. She found herself obliged to wash in the bedroom at a washstand equipped with a porcelain toilet set, complete with chamber pot, and to bathe in a hip-bath filled from a bucket.

According to James Pope Hennessy's biography of Stevenson, Fanny later confessed to her mother-in-law that she had not been able to lift the heavy ewer in her bedroom and assumed that: "Heriot Row lacked wash-basins and running water because her parents-in-law could not afford such normal transatlantic comforts." If she had come a few years later she would have found something quite different. The late Victorian bathroom and perfectly preserved bath still in use at 17 Heriot Row, now the home of Lord and Lady Dunpark, show that comfortable Edinburgh families were at last beginning to make full use of the latest technology.

The dressing-room next to the master bedroom was now equipped with a flushing water-closet (still decently tucked away in a cupboard) which drained efficiently, and a full size, plumbed-in bath with large-bore shining brass taps. Directly above the taps and plug hole a wooden shower head was fitted into a cupboard containing a water tank. To operate the shower the bather pulled a string.

Opposite and above: *The bathroom at 17 Heriot Row:*
1 The Victorian zinc bath "built to cosset the human body" with original brass taps and fittings. 2 Fanny Stevenson might well have worn a silk dressing cape like this while attending her toilette. 3 Contents of the cupboard. Did Robert Louis Stevenson have recourse to the Sloan's Liniment after a day on the Pentland Hills? 4 General view of the bathroom, painted light blue in the belief that it kept flies away. A Nannie's dress in rough cotton with horn buttons hangs appropriately here, in the house which inspired 'A Child's Garden of Verses'.

And that wasn't all. The 1892 catalogue published by Wood & Cairns, plumbers' merchants still operating in Edinburgh, offers an extraordinary range of ways to keep clean. As well as showers, shampoo taps and douches there was an attachment sadly lacking in modern bathrooms: the spray, a clever arrangement of pipes which played jets of hot or cold water onto your body while you stood in the bath. The spray was built into a raised hood at the tap end of the bath, which looked a little like an Orkney chair.

Perhaps the most surprising thing is that it took so long for the benefits of plumbing and running water to work their way into the British home. The Stevensons were not at all unusual in their way of life. The bathroom as we know it represents a triumph of technology which was not fully achieved until towards the end of the nineteenth century. You could catch a train from London to Edinburgh in 1847, making use of the best engineering advances of the time, but you might find it much harder ro run a bath or flush the W.C.

The comparatively slow development of the British bathroom depended partly on conquering the technical difficulties of piping large quantities of fresh water into city homes and draining dirty water safely out again without polluting the drinking water supply. But there were social reasons too. There was no great urgency for technology when there were enough servants in even quite modest homes to carry out the more unpleasant tasks connected with keeping people clean. The comfort and hygiene we take for granted at the turn of a tap or flush of the pan depended on maids carrying buckets of clean water upstairs and dirty commodes downstairs.

Although a flushing water-closet much as we use today had been invented by Joseph Bramah as early as 1778, many homes often still preferred earth closets or commodes. Until plumbing and water supply could be relied on, it was less offensive to have an outside privy or frequently emptied commode than a smelly, perhaps leaky, water closet. Besides, there was money to be made from the vast quantities of night soil produced in growing cities. Every evening Leerie, the Lamplighter, stopped to light the lamp outside 17 Heriot Row. Every morning another man, who does not appear in Stevenson's *A Child's Garden of Verses,* called to fill the cart with night soil from the house to sell to market gardens on the city's outskirts.

In 1871 Edinburgh was reported to have one water-closet for every six people, compared with Perth's one in thirty-three and Aberdeen's one in forty-four. But the number of wealthy homes with more than one convenience pushed up the city's average. Baths and water-closets had been used in large country houses from the eighteenth century, sometimes with their own fresh water piped or pumped in, sometimes flushed none too reliably by the rain. Difficulties were greater in the cities, where the new water authorities could not keep up with increasing demands for fresh water from a rapidly growing population.

Families like the Stevensons who could afford to buy a bath very likely did not bother while the water supply was unreliable. By the end of the 1880s the Edinburgh and District Water Trustees were claiming to be able to supply the whole city and, to judge from the Wood & Cairns catalogue, the 'sanitary trade' began to expand and prosper. You could buy a plate zinc bath six feet long, very much like the Rufford of Stockbridge model at 17 Heriot Row, for £3 10s 6d; or one four feet long, 'suitable for workmen's house' for £2 10s (about a week's wage). A portable bath on wheels was made

for hospitals, 'price on request'. Lady Dunpark, formerly Councillor Kathleen McFie, says that the baths were "built to cosset the human body, broader at the shoulder end, narrow at the feet and tapering in at the base so they could be filled deep without using too much water".

At first the room itself was kept fairly plain, a dressing room with plumbing, painted buff or, like the Dunpark's, light blue in the belief that it kept flies away - the grand scale of deliberately designed bathrooms did not emerge until 1900. But the fittings were designed with a decorative care which shows a craftsmanlike approach to manufacturing, a fascination with the working of things. On rising from the Best Bramah Closet, or presumably even better, the Superior Bramah Closet, you could reach up and grasp a brass fist to flush the bowl, perhaps lavishly decorated with flowers. You could run a bath from the mouth of a lion's head and any overflow escaped through a decorative brass grating.

Wood & Cairns, founded in 1790 as brass founders and gas fitters under the name of Hume & Melville, were supplying baths and Bramah closets across Scotland from the 1860s, but the real expansion took place in the 1890s when growth in the business brought about an important change. From now on, according to the secretary's notes for 1893, W.C. seats made by the joiner were superseded by those made by machine. There can be a price to pay for progress, as even Fanny Stevenson might have agreed.

Illustrations from Wood & Cairns's 1892 Catalogue.

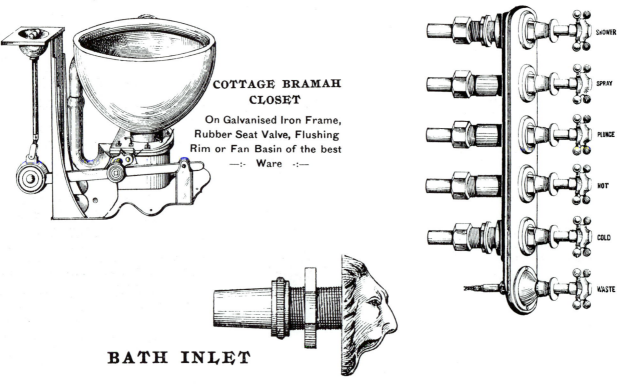

COTTAGE BRAMAH CLOSET

On Galvanised Iron Frame, Rubber Seat Valve, Flushing Rim or Fan Basin of the best —:- Ware -:—

BATH INLET

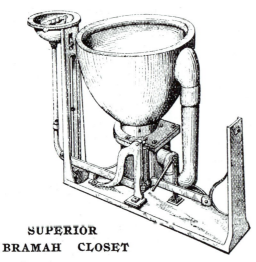

SUPERIOR BRAMAH CLOSET

On Galvanised Iron Frame, Stuffing Box on Axle Bush, Rubber Seat Valve, Flushing Rim or Fan Basin ———— of the best Ware ————

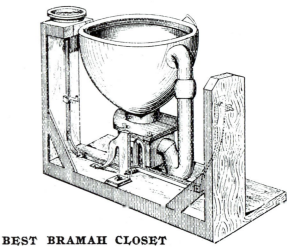

BEST BRAMAH CLOSET

On Wood Frame, Stuffing Box on Axle Bush, Gun Metal Ground Valve, Flushing Rim or Fan Basin of the ———— best Ware ————